Mysteries and Miracles
of Arizona

By Jack Kutz

Rhombus Publishing Company

Rhombus Publishing Company, Inc.
P.O. Box 806, Corrales, New Mexico 87048

To Michael

Contents

Foreword

When I was a kid back in the 1930s, my favorite aunt kept a rainbow in a jar.

It was a small, clear glass vial set on a little pedestal, filled with carefully sifted layers of colored sand from the Painted Desert. My aunt had only been to Arizona once in her life, and her "rainbow" was her only souvenir. But, she never forgot that trip and she talked about it often.

She would tell me about the immensity of the Grand Canyon, about great rock formations that looked like the heads of giants, and sunsets that seemed to set the clouds on fire. She told me there was even a petrified forest where, she swore, petrified birds perched and sang petrified songs.

To a young, impressionable boy growing up in the Nebraska flatlands, Arizona sounded like a wonderful place, and I could hardly wait until I would be old enough to see it for myself. When that time came, it was just like Auntie said it would be, even though —as

I always suspected, there were no petrified birds. From that time on, I traveled to Arizona as often as possible. After my wife, La Donna, our children, and I moved to the Southwest in 1962, I began to absorb the mystery and majesty of the deserts, the mountain forests, the intrigue of the long-vanished Indian civilizations, the awesome power of their descendants, the Hopis, the Navajo, the legends of lost treasure, the eerie tales of the supernatural and the strange, but well-documented, stories of extra-terrestrial visitations.

There is something magical about the entire Southwest; some sort of wondrously spooky allurement exists here —a psychic magnet that draws star-crossed people from all parts of the world to unexpected but inevitable destinies.

Many of these special mortals were part of great migrations, while others were lonely wanderers, seekers and searchers, fugitives and lost souls. And a good many of them were already living in Arizona, unknowingly awaiting the incredible events that would interrupt and forever change their lives.

Yet, in every instance, their stories —even the most recent ones— are almost completely forgotten. What I have tried to do in this book is to rescue these tales from oblivion, to present them as accurately as possible, for the first time in a single volume.

To do so, I spent an uncounted number of very pleasant hours wandering the aisles of libraries around the Southwest. I owe a special thanks to the gracious librarians in cities and small towns who helped me obtain the information herein, and who responded so promptly to my requests for inter-library loan service.

I am even more indebted to the people with whom I had extensive correspondence, people who I never met in person, but who all seemed to share my enthusiasm for this unusual book project.

And best of all, are my memories of the folks I met along the way: old timers in desert campgrounds telling tales over early-morning coffee, the Navajo caretakers of the sacred animals in Window Rock, the intensely serene New Agers of Sedona, and many others.

The mysteries in this book span the ages, from prehistory to the present day, and they are as varied as the Arizona landscape itself. However, this book is intended to be more than just a collection of strange stories. It is a guidebook offering specific directions to readers who may wish to follow my path in exploring these mysteries.

Mysteries and Miracles of Arizona is an invitation to curious, insightful thinkers and cynical skeptics alike to personally explore the old legends, to probe the wavering lines between fact, fiction and fantasy that arise like shimmering mirages in the Arizona desert.

Arizona is both a place and a state of mind, a land where flute music can bring rain, where snakes carry messages to the gods, sandstone can breathe —and where rainbows can be captured in jars.

1

The Roman Swords
of Silverbell Road

Every desert has a thousand stories to tell.

Sometimes, the stories are revealed in petroglyphs pecked into rocks by ancient Indians in special places. Flint knives and arrowheads tell tales of hunting and warfare, while pottery shards speak of artistry and craftsmanship. Old glass bottles, blue with age, rusting Prince Albert tins, discarded horseshoes, abandoned mine shafts —each and everyone has a story behind it.

One can never be sure which chapter of its history a desert will present next to one of its visitors, nor when it will give some passerby a glimpse of one of its many well-kept secrets. Certainly, one of the desert's strangest revelations was made, quite unexpectedly, to a couple of Sunday afternoon strollers in the autumn of 1924 on the outskirts of Tucson.

Charles Manier, a Tuscon resident, was entertaining an out-of-state guest, a cousin from back East. Together, they drove out on Silverbell Road which was then the edge of town. Manier parked on the shoulder and set the handbrake. "Down there," he pointed, "are some old Spanish lime kilns. I think you'll find them interesting. Come. Let's take a walk."

The two gentlemen clamored unsteadily down the embankment, with Manier balancing himself on his metal-tipped cane. When they reached the bottom of the arroyo which led to the crumbling kilns, Manier gestured at the eroded slope. "Perfect example here of exposed desert stratus," he observed. "See how the arroyo has cut through the layers of soil? I imagine if we were to do a bit of digging, up there near the surface, we might very well turn up an early Spanish relic or two. Just below that, I expect we'd find a few pieces of Indian pottery. And down here at this level —who knows?"

He tapped what appeared to be a protruding rock with his cane, and the "rock" gave off a dull metalic ring. "Now what do you suppose that could be?" Manier asked his cousin. "Wait here. I have some tools in the car. It won't take long to dig that thing out."

Charles Manier scrambled back up the embankment, opened his tool box, and took out a short-handled shovel which he, like most desert travelers, always carried in those days. He scurried back down to his cousin, and the two of them took turns hacking away at the rock-hard caliche in which the object was embedded. The encrusted piece of metal was much larger than expected; more than an hour passed before it would be wrested from the slope and plopped on the ground.

The object was long and narrow with what appeared to be a handgrip at the top above a broad, oval-shaped flange. It was so heavy that it took both men to lug it up to the car and slide in onto the floor boards. "I know the man who owns this land," Manier said as he started the engine. "His name's Thomas Bent. Let's drive over to his house. I'm sure he'd like to see whatever it is we've got here."

Thomas Bent was indeed interested in the curious object. He helped Manier and his cousin clean off the last of the dirt, beneath which there was a coating of beeswax. When the hardened wax had been peeled away, they found themselves staring at a distinctively shaped, crudely molded piece of lead. "A sword," Manier said. "I'll be damned. It's a sword."

"Two swords," Bent corrected him. "They've been pressed together and joined with metal dowels. Let's see if we can separate them." Using as much care as possible, Bent removed the dowels, pried the swords apart, and turned them over. After brushing them off, an inscription in a foreign language appeared. Its letters covered the flanges beneath the handles and extended down the blades.

"The swords of Spanish explorers!" Manier exclaimed.

Bent shook his head. "Not unless they knew how to write Latin. As an attorney, I am somewhat familiar with that particular language. I can assure you this is Latin, not Spanish." He traced his finger across the inscription. "Look at these words: 'Roman Terra Calalus'."

"But... that's utterly impossible!" Manier protested. "Roman swords in Arizona? How did they get here? And when? And why would anyone make a sword out of lead in the first place?"

Bent stood up and brushed off his knees. "Charles," he said, "those questions will have to be answered by someone much more knowledgeable than we."

A few days later, Bent took the artifacts to the University of Arizona where he showed them to the staff of the Department of Archaeology. The astonished archaeologists were almost speechless at first. They listened to Bent's story about the discovery, examined the objects with an unconcealed sense of disbelief, and quickly and unanimously agreed on one thing: "This *must* be shown to Dr. Cummings."

Dr. Byron Cummings was one of the most highly-respected Southwestern archaeologists of his time and was commonly regarded as the leading specialist in the pre-history of Arizona. He was then working at an archaeological dig in Mexico, but when news of the Tucson find reached him, he hastened back to Arizona. He studied the swords carefully, confirming first that the inscriptions were unquestionably Latin, and therefore easily translatable. However, he was much more intrigued by the strange drawings scratched upon the second sword.

The stem of this relic was topped by a broad, flat ellipsis, shaped much like a paddle on the end of an oar. Near the top, a crown and two swords had been drawn. The swords were poised at right angles above five adjoining squares criss-crossed by vertical and

DESCRIPTIONS OF VANISHED TERRA CALALUS. A crown, two swords, and architectural illustrations are inscribed on an artifact unearthed outside Tucson.

Desert Magazine Archives

diagonal lines which formed a geometric pattern open to any number of interpretations. Beneath this design was carefully-etched depiction of what appeared to be a round, domed temple supported by a circle of columns.

Byron Cummings was not a man who jumped to conclusions or made hasty judgements, but this time, he was so excited by what he was seeing that he promptly pronounced the artifacts to be Roman/ Byzantine in style and furthermore —if they were genuine— they were on a par with the Rosetta Stone which unlocked the secrets of Egyptian hieroglyphics in 1799. Cumming's report on the find caught the attention of the *New York Times*. A front page story, complete with photographs, soon appeared, and dozens of people who had an interest in antiquities began calling Dr. Cummings.

The curator of American Archaeology of the United States National Museum, Neil M. Judd, said he believed the relics to be authentic and surmised they were probably older than the Spanish conquest of 1540. Dr. Bradford Dean, curator of arms and armor of New York's Metropolitan Museum, felt sure the whole thing was a hoax though he could not explain how or why the deception was perpetrated. A retired Mexican rancher, Leandro Ruiz, thought he might have the answer. In the 1890s, he had known the family of Mexican immigrants who lived on the land before Thomas Bent purchased it. Perhaps one of his mischievous sons made the swords and buried them, he suggested.

After a team of geologists visited the site, they dismissed this theory. According to Dr. C.J. Saria, the layer of calcium carbonate that had dried into near-stone had never been disturbed from above. If the objects actually came from this layer of caliche, they had rested there for several centuries.

Cummings and other members of the university's archaeology department knew that a comprehensive dig should be conducted on the site as soon as possible. Unfortunately, no funds for such a project were available. Thomas Bent, who yearned as much as anyone to see the mystery solved, offered a proposal. He volunteered to personally finance an excavation if the university would agree to give him a share of the profits when the relics they expected to uncover were sold to museums. In the event that nothing of value was found, the university would reimburse Bent for his expenses when its budget permitted it to do so.

The young attorney drew up a contract, Cummings happily signed it, and the digging began.

At a depth of two to three feet, the excavators unearthed a number of common pre-Columbian artifacts: arrowheads, flint knives and bits of pottery. Soon, they entered the caliche layer, using extreme caution as they dug. Before long, the archaeologists' efforts were rewarded by the discovery of a small crescent cross. This find, in itself, appeared to justify their faith in the project.

But there was more to come.

Metal spearheads began turning up, along with a serpent cross and more swords. Perhaps the most remarkable object to emerge from the aged, dried mud was a small replica of a labarum —the royal cavalry standard carried in front of Roman emperors in war. All told, the site yielded 32 artifacts. Although some were merely fragments, enough bore legible inscriptions for Cummings to piece together an epic story.

According to Cumming's translation, a great fleet of ships carrying 700 Romans under the command of Theodorus the Renowned set sail from Rome in 775

A.D. This proud flotilla passed through the Straits of Hercules into the open Atlantic. Here, the ships were hit by a series of violent storms which drove the fleet far off course. Most of the vessels had been swamped and sunk. The survivors finally reached calm waters in what was probably the Gulf of Mexico. They drifted westward until they could go no further by sea. Somewhere along the coast of what is now Texas, the Romans disembarked and headed inland until they reached the place where their relics were found.

Under the direction of Theodorus, they built a city and named it Terra Calalus. Being Romans, they wanted slaves, so they captured and subjugated a large number of local Indians. Eventually, the Indians rebelled, slew Theodorus and regained their freedom. Now the diminished colony came under the leadership of Jacobus, who was later succeeded by Israel I. Under Israel I, the enslaving of Indians was forcibly reintroduced. Terra Calalus flourished for more than a hundred years.

At last, in 900 A.D., there was a second slave rebellion which ended in the near-total defeat of the descendants of the original Roman settlers. Israel VII ordered his scribe to record the story of Terra Calalus on ceremonial swords made of lead, had them interred near the city and, then apparently abandoned the site. What happened to the colonists after that, only the desert itself knows.

Dr. Cummings completed his examination of the relics by having samples of the lead analyzed. He learned the metal was a fairly sophisticated alloy hardened with antimony. Two of the better crafted pieces contained copper of a type similar to ore found near Bisbee, 100 miles southeast of the Silverbell site.

Confident that the artifacts were authentic, Cummings made his findings public, then braced himself for the storm of controversy he knew would follow. He realized he was challenging one of American's most cherished myths, since he was about to prove that Christopher Columbus was not the first European to discover the Western Hemisphere. If, on the other hand, he failed to convince his fellow archaeologists, he knew he would seriously damage his own academic reputation and bring nothing but scorn and ridicule upon himself.

The initial reaction of the scientific community was largely favorable. Several of the experts who had been skeptical of the original discovery now congratulated Dr. Cummings on a job well done. Still, many archaeologists and historians continued to scoff and to insist the whole matter was nothing but an elaborate hoax. When word leaked out about the financial arrangement between Thomas Bent and the Department of Archaeology, the critics raised a cry of fraud. They accused Bent of creating phony artifacts and burying them on his land in the hope of making a rather handsome profit when the bogus relics were sold. Dr. Cummings was denounced as being either naive and gullible or, worse yet, a collaborator in the swindle.

Cumming's students, who had participated in the dig and helped uncover, lift out and brush off the heavily-encrusted objects, rose in defense of their professor. They swore the caliche showed no signs of prior intrusion, and there was simply no way the artifacts could have been secretly planted five to six feet below the surface of the ground. Bent was equally offended by the charges. He wrote a lengthy report detailing precisely how the dig had been conducted, sending copies to universities and museums around the country. But it was all in vain; the project's credibility was already damaged beyond repair.

The University of Arizona was acutely embarrassed by the scandal and wished only to sweep the whole mess under the rug as quickly as possible. Dr. Cummings was relieved of his faculty position; the objects themselves were given back to Bent. Thomas Bent kept them in his possession until he died in the 1970s, at which time they were given to his son.

Were the Roman artifacts genuine? Is the story of Terra Calalus true? Nearly seven decades have passed since Charles Manier took his cousin for a Sunday drive on Tucson's Silverbell Road. During the years that have gone by, an intriguing number of pre-Columbian antiquities have turned up in other parts of the country, enough to make the Tucson discovery worthy of further speculation.

Roman coins have shown up in a variety of locations throughout the South and in New England. Often they were deep inside earthen Indian mounds, but many were spaded up accidently by gardeners, farmers and construction workers. Some were found beneath the roots of 300- to 400-year-old trees. Farther west, coins appeared in Michigan, Ohio and Arkansas, Texas, Colorado and Wyoming. In all of these areas, the soils have yielded up the poorly-minted pocket change of ancient Rome.

Fascinating as these coins are, they were sometimes accompanied by even more interesting objects... things like Roman lamps, goblets, vases and knife blades. In nearly every case, the authenticity of these odd antiques proved unquestionable. Even when there was room for doubt, the possibility that they could actually be of Roman origin remained. But how did they get here? Who brought them, and when?

Dr. Barry Fell has spent a substantial part of his life attempting to answer vexing questions of this sort. Professor emeritus at Harvard and president of the Epigraphic Society, Dr. Fell has been examining archaeological sites in the United States, British Columbia, the Mediterranean countries and northern Africa for more than a quarter of a century. The primary purpose of his never-ending research is to prove that multitudes of peoples from many distant lands crossed the seas and explored the Americas from coast to coast centuries before Columbus' voyage. The evidence Fell has amassed is, to say the least, rather astonishing.

According to Dr. Fell, the earliest visits occurred long before the birth of Christ and increased dramatically during the first few centuries A.D. Seafarers from Phoenicia, Greece, Lybia, Scandanavia and even China repeatedly sailed from the Old Worlds to the New. Apparently the Celts of northern Italy began arriving at least as early as 400 B.C. A coin bearing the head of Hercules on one side and a depiction of the gorgon Medusa on the other was plowed out of the ground by an Ohio farmer in 1880. In the 1970s, Dr. Fell examined this half-dollar sized disc and found it identical to a Celtibarian coin widely circulated in what is now Italy during the late 4th century B.C.

The presence of coins in an archaeological dig often provides an easy means of dating the site. Roman coins usually bore the likeness of the current emperor, along with his exalted name. On the coins found in North America, each successive emperor from Antonius Pius (138-383 A.D.) to Gratianus (367-383 A.D.) has been represented. The heaviest concentrations of Roman antiquities appeared on and near the eastern and southern seacoasts but became fewer in number throughout the land that sprawls out to the west.

By tracing a tenuous line between the widely-separated sites, Fell and many of his colleagues came to believe there had once been a transcontinental track which extended all the way from the eastern shores to the Pacific Northwest. The routes of these explorations seem not to have crossed Arizona, yet only in Arizona has tangible evidence of a permanent settlement been uncovered. If there really was a Terra Calalus, it was surely the most remote outpost of the Roman empire, and it obviously came into existence quite by accident.

Clearly Theodorus the Renowned never intended to wind up in the Gulf of Mexico. But once there, it would have seemed practical for him to build his settlement on the coast of Texas. Instead, he led his party inland for more than a thousand miles before he decided to go no further. Since he traveled in a northwesterly direction, it may be safe to assume he hoped to intersect the Roman's cross-country trail and link up with other European explorers. By the time he reached south-central Arizona, he may have realized this was an impossible goal.

If Theodorus sent out advance scouts, they could only have brought back bad news, for the country that lay ahead was even more desolate than the lands they had already crossed. The Italian explorer's decision to establish a colony near the banks of the Santa Cruz River seems quite logical under the circumstances.

When Charles Manier tapped his cane on what he thought was an ordinary rock, he was knocking on the doors of antiquity. Thomas Bent and Byron Cummings opened those doors barely a crack. The site they excavated was surely only a small corner of this mini-civilization which apparently lasted more than one hundred years. The desert tried to reveal this strange, hidden secret, but no one was ready to look. And now it is too late.

How to Visit Terra Calalus

What kind of city was Terra Calalus? Were there fields and orchards, quarries and mines in which generations of slaves toiled under the lash? Was there really a domed temple supported by stone pillars? When one drives Tucson's Silverbell Road today, it is hard to believe there may be Roman artifacts and relics beneath the pavement of this bustling thoroughfare, or under the banks of the shallow river that parallels it. But somewhere below this busy street lined with mobile homes, gas stations and small shops may lie the sites of ancient battlefields where desperate slaves fought against their cruel masters; there may be cemeteries where a succession of pretentious monarchs are entombed near crumbled altars. But Silverbell Road today offers no clues.

Bibliography - Chapter 1

Esplin, Lola. *Desert* magazine, March 1981.

Fell, Barry. **Saga America.** Times Books. New York 1980.

Pepper, Choral. *Desert* magazine, December 1980.

Richey, Clifford C. *Desert* magazine, March 1981.

Trento, Salvatore Michael. **The Search for Lost America.** Contemporary Books, Chicago 1978.

2

Curse of the
Superstition Mountains

Rarely has anyone been at a loss for words when asked to describe the Superstition Mountains of Arizona. "Awesome" is usually the first word uttered, followed by "stark, harsh, and scary." These forbidding peaks have been called "the most savage piece of land in North America, a stone maze built by the Apache Thunder God." Or, as an old prospector once put it: "Walk in for thirty minutes and you will be in the slag dumps of Hell."

The Superstitions are utterly inhospitable. They are unbearably hot in summer and, except for a few rock potholes and rare springs, dry as bones. The spiny vegetation that clings to the hillsides and chokes the canyons is as unfriendly as anything that grows: thickets of catclaw acacia, ocotillo and burrobush, forests of stately saguaros, tree-sized chollas and rotund, barbed barrel cactus.

The rock formations are downright eerie —rows upon rows of tall, stone columns which the Pima Indians believed were unfortunate wanderers turned to stone by angry gods who caught them trespassing. It doesn't take much imagination to see human faces on many of the columns, especially when the shadows are just right.

Today these grand, desolate mountains are permanently protected as a congressionally-designated, 240-square-mile federal wilderness area, a place where, in the words of the Wilderness Act of 1964, "man himself is a visitor who does not remain." That seems appropriate for the Superstitions: over the centuries many men have gone in, but none remained for long.

It could be said that the Superstition Mountains have been somewhat like a stage: empty most of the time, but visited frequently by actors and actresses who played out brief dramas and were soon gone. The players on this vast, geologic stage were as fascinating a cast of characters as any playwright could hope to conjure.

No two were alike; all were as different as their costumes. Some wore the proud sombreros of Mexico while others bound their black, wind-tangled hair with Indian headbands. A number of them shaded their faces with dirty, sweat-stained prospectors' hats. At least one may have worn the blue coat and yellow-striped pants of an Army medical officer, while another preferred the long, black coat, white collar and cravat of an aristocrat.

One of the more mysterious was a dark-skinned woman who usually had a full-length shawl drawn around her shoulders. It was said she was well-prac-

THE SUPERSTITION MOUNTAINS. Which of the pinnacles in "the most savage piece of land in North America" have a core of pure gold?

Photo by Jack Kutz

ticed in the occult and could see images in fire that others could not. If anyone could perceive the curse on the Superstitions, it was probably she.

As diverse as these people were, they did nonetheless, have much in common. Each was sure that he or she was the only person destined to succeed where all others had failed at their quixotic search for the mountains' fabulous treasure. Most were doomed to fail and nearly all would come to strange, tragic ends.

The curtain rose on this drama in 1840 when a man named Don Miguel Peralta de Cordova led an expedition into the Superstitions. All of the land his pack train crossed had belonged to his family for three generations. The Peralta Land Grant had been bestowed upon Don Luís María Peralta by King Ferdinand VII of Spain in 1748. It extended all the way from the trail junction that would someday become the city of Phoenix to the Continental Divide, where the town of Silver City, New Mexico, now stands... in all, some 18,000 square miles of largely unexplored wilderness.

The king's generosity was graciously accepted but little appreciated. Luís Peralta and his brother, Manuel, already had huge land holdings in Spanish California where they were in the process of establishing several very profitable cattle ranches and silver mines. A distant tract of barren desert was of little interest to them. No one from the Peralta families bothered to visit this generally forgotten domain for nearly a hundred years.

Then, finally, the grandsons of Manuel Peralta decided to take a look at this long-neglected royal gift. They were adventurous young men and not unwilling to endure a few hardships or take a few risks. Undoubtedly, they found the country to be wilder than they expected but they proceeded undaunted into the mighty Superstition range to do a little prospecting.

It would seem an unlikely place to find gold. The mountains are volcanic in origin, and lava-rock is almost always without precious mineral potential. Still, when molten lava bursts through the surface of the earth, there's no telling what it may bring up with it. A gold deposit in a geologic layer far beneath the ground can spew up upward in a jet of red-hot magma which hardens in a vertical vein as it cools. It doesn't happen often, but it can.

The Peralta brothers must have felt themselves extremely lucky to find traces of placer gold almost right away, flecks and specks which led them uphill to a larger deposit. There, they set their peons to work digging out a mine, crushing the ore and separating the gold from the common rock. The Peraltas' first expedition did not bring out a fortune, but it was more than enough to draw them back again. And again.

Over the years, they established at least eight gold mines in the Superstitions. But although these rather small-scale operations were yielding reasonable profits, they were high-risk enterprises. The cruel desert environment was not the only enemy they faced each time they returned to their mines. The Apaches, for example, had never heard of a Spanish land grant. The absurd notion that the flourish of a feathery pen in a faraway royal court could rob them of their ancestral lands was hardly a laughing matter. The nomadic Apaches believed they and they alone owned all the land they rode across. Anyone who thought otherwise was in for trouble.

The Peraltas' first skirmishes with the Apaches were minor ones... sporadic sniper fire from concealed positions high in the rocks and the occasional theft of a burro or two. It was just enough harassment to make the miners wonder whether it was worth risking their lives for a relatively modest financial return. Then one day, probably in 1845, Don Miguel Peralta found something that made the risk well worth taking. Somewhere in that enormous snarl of jagged rocks, he hit the mother lode.

Most contemporary researchers agree it was a "chimney lode" —a wide, vertical vein of pure gold encased in a rose-colored quartz shaft so deep that only the devil himself knew its true depth. The miners immediately began digging. Within a remarkably short time, they had loaded up all the gold their burros could carry. They hurriedly left the Superstitions, and, though the Apaches encouraged their departure by taking pot-shots at them, they vowed to return.

When they reached civilization, however, they learned that their future, and that of the entire Southwest, was about to change forever. The Mexican-American War had just begun. When it ended in 1847, all the land north of Chihuahua and Sonora was ceded to the United States by the Treaty of Guadalupe-Hidalgo. The treaty contained a provision that protected the rights of the Hispanic land grantees, but Miguel Peralta was wise enough to know that when the Anglos learned how rich his mining claim was, they would find a way to steal it. The only thing to do, he reasoned, was to head back to the mountains as soon as he could and pack out as much gold as possible. In 1848, he made his last trip into the Superstitions.

The caravan he led was his largest ever, consisting of as many as 50 men and pack animals. Miguel Peralta took his sons along this time, even though they must have been quite young for such a perilous adventure. He easily relocated his diggings, set up a camp, and everyone went to work.

They had labored no more than a few days before the Apaches made their presence known. A burro disappeared from the mining party's corral one night, and its hide and bones were found the next afternoon beside the campfire ashes where it had been roasted and eaten. Peralta was not too concerned; he probably felt one burro was a small price to pay if it kept the Apaches happy. If he wondered how many Indians it took to eat an entire burro, it didn't take long to find out.

During the next few days, Apaches began appearing everywhere, silhouetted on the ridge tops and riding openly in large numbers across the bed of the canyon below the mine. Everyday there seemed to be more of them. Clearly, it was high time to pack up the gold and get the hell out of the Superstitions. The miners were hurriedly breaking camp and loading the burros when the Apaches struck.

Many versions relate the massacre that followed, but it is safe to say that the first volley of bullets and arrows knocked down several men and that the rest dove into the rocks from which they could defend themselves. The Apaches' siege probably lasted three days as the Indians selectively, almost leisurely, picked off the miners, one by one.

Then, on the fourth day, the sun rose over an ominously quiet scene. Survivors cautiously lifted their heads and hesitantly stepped out into the open. The Apaches were gone. Many men dropped to their knees, crossed themselves and sobbed a prayer of thanks. But Miguel Peralta simply reloaded his rifle. *"Ahora, nosotros corremos la baqueta,"* he said, "Now, we run the gauntlet."

Peralta knew it would be suicidal to head back

out the way they had come in, so he led his men into a different ravine. How far the packtrain got before it was ambushed is uncertain, but it seems clear the Apaches were not fooled by the change of route. The first barrage seemed to come from all directions at once, and Peralta knew instantly that everyone was doomed.

In the last moments of his life, he pushed his sons into a deep crevice in the rocks and made a frantic dash down the canyon to draw the Indians away from the hiding place. He was quickly shot down, along with all the others.

It may have been days before the two boys dared to creep out of the rocks. Miraculously, they managed to slip undetected through this hostile territory until they reached the Salt River and safety. At this point in their lives, the boys probably never wanted to see those dreadful mountains again. They were too young to know that the Superstitions never let go of anyone.

Many years passed before any Peraltas re-entered the story. In the meantime, others had roles to play upon this haunted stage. The next was a man who was literally forced to play his part. His name was Abraham Thorne. Some accounts say he was the post surgeon at Fort McDowell; others contend he was a doctor in private practice. Either way, he had gained a reputation for his willingness to treat Indian patients.

Dr. Thorne was highly respected in the Pima settlements along the Verde River where he spent considerable time helping a people badly in need of basic medical care. As word of his good deeds spread, the Apaches grew envious. They, too, could use the services of an altruistic physician. At that time, they were also well aware that they were totally unwelcome outside their own strongholds. So, they decided, if they couldn't go to the doctor, the doctor would have to

come to them. One day in 1860 or '61, they simply kidnapped Dr. Thorne as he was returning from a Pima
village.

Blindfolded and stuck on a horse, he was taken
to a camp deep in the Superstitions. The doctor had no
choice but to accept his new practice. During the
months that followed, he treated the Apaches for everything from trachoma to gangrene.

Then, one day, he told his captors he had done
all he could. It was time for him to return to his own
people. The Apaches accepted his decision and, once
again, a bandana was tied over his eyes and he was
hoisted onto a horse. The doctor had no way of judging
how many miles they rode before the Apaches stopped
and removed the blindfold. Squinting against the sudden glare, he saw they had halted in a narrow canyon
strewn with the bones of burros. The Apaches gestured
for him to dismount, and when he had done so, they
urged him to look around. Thorne must have thought
the heat was causing him to hallucinate, for everywhere he looked, he saw heaps of gold nuggets. Beside
each skeleton were the contents of the canvas sacks
that had been these unfortunate animals' last burdens.
The Indians made scooping motions and pointed to
Thorne's saddle bags, making it clear that this was
their way of paying their doctor bills.

Thorne eagerly stuffed his saddle bags to their
limits and, after a moment's hesitation, he pulled off
his pants, tied them into a two-legged sack and filled
them with nuggets also. Then, with the blindfold
secure once more, he got back on the horse and the
journey was resumed. The Indians continued for two
full days, removing the blindfold only at night when
they camped. On the morning of the third day, Thorne
awoke to find himself alone; the Apaches had slipped

away just before dawn. The campsite where they left their benefactor had been well-chosen. There was a tiny mountain stream nearby which Thorne was able to follow until he reached the Verde River. Late that afternoon, a very happy, very rich, and very sunburned doctor rode into Fort McDowell.

Abraham Thorne has the distinction of being the only person whom the Superstition Mountains treated kindly, but, in a sense, he, too, was cursed. Though he was now comfortably wealthy, he could not forget how much gold he had left behind. He knew he had to go back and he was pretty sure he knew where to go. While the blindfold was off, Thorne had caught a glimpse of a tall, vertical peak beyond the canyon, a sharp volcanic fang standing alone in the Superstitions' wildly chaotic landscape. It was shimmering in the heat wave, so he could not judge its distance, nor its height, but it was so distinctive he firmly believed he could find it again. He was sure that once he had located that landmark, he could rediscover the canyon where the Peralta burros had been slain.

Dr. Thorne organized a group of friends into an expedition which headed off toward the notorious peaks. Weeks later they returned without having come anywhere near the elusive pinnacle. Thorne spent some more of his fortune to outfit a second group of searchers. This time, they came in from the south, as Peralta had done, and, within hours, rode up to the base of the towering rock formation known today as the Weaver's Needle.

This austere spire is the grandest feature of the entire mountain range. It stands atop a huge earthen pedestal like a dark sentinel guarding the labyrinthian kingdom that surrounds it. From the Weaver's Needle, canyons and their tributaries claw the land for miles in every direction. Thorne and his friends soon found out how difficult it is to search that kind of terrain. They rode up and down as many canyons as they could before they ran out of supplies. Finally they had to straggle back home empty-handed.

But the good doctor refused to give up: he made several more trips into the mountains, but failed to find a trace of the treasure. It is possible, of course, that the Apaches themselves removed the gold and hid it elsewhere, just as they may have filled in Peralta's mine and covered it over. If so, they did a good job, because Thorne became so frustrated by his wasted efforts that he finally lost his mind. Unfortunate as this was, there were greater tragedies to come. Now it was time for the play's leading man to make his appearance.

This player had come all the way from Germany where he had been born in 1810. His name was Jacob Walz, and his nickname was "Deutsch." On the Southwestern frontier, he came to be known as Jacob "Dutch" Walz, but posthumously he would always be referred to as "The Dutchman."

A veteran of hard-rock gold prospecting in California, Walz was already in his fifties when he drifted into Arizona in 1862. During the next few years, he filed several small claims in the Prescott area, but none of them proved to be commercially workable. Then, in 1870, he formed a partnership with a man named Jacob Weiser, and his luck changed dramatically.

Walz and Weiser, like everyone else in the Arizona Territory, had heard tales of the Peralta mine and Dr. Thorne's half-mad quest. If such an enormous bonanza really was out there somewhere in those hellish mountains, they figured it would take experienced prospectors like themselves to find it. These two men knew just about everything there was to know about the primitive 19th century art of searching for gold in unlikely places. Yet in spite of their talents, neither man had ever made a really big strike. They were both getting on in years; they understood that unless they hit real pay-dirt soon, they never would. Into the Superstitions they went.

For one of them, it was the best decision he ever made. For the other, it was the worst.

No one knows how long it took them to find the old Peralta mine, but apparently, through skill or blind luck, they did. One day they showed up in the fledgling town of Phoenix leading two mules loaded with pouches filled with gold. They filed no claim and refused to talk about where they had been. They simply bought more provisions, a couple extra mules and rode out of town, disappearing into the Superstitions.

Weeks later they came back out, hauling twice as much gold as before. This time, however, they had a tale to tell.

They said they had set up camp a short distance downhill from their mine. Early one morning when Walz hiked up to the diggings, he was surprised to hear voices. He crept closer and saw two brown-skinned men picking up rocks at the entrance to the mine. Walz immediately dashed back to camp and motioned to Weiser. "Apaches! Get your rifle and come with me."

The two men ran in a crouch up the hillside, positioning themselves in the rocks. Taking careful aim, they shot both of the unsuspecting intruders. When they rolled the bodies over, they found the men that had killed were Mexicans, not Apaches. Reckoning these would-be claim-jumpers had followed them all the way from Phoenix, the old prospectors must have felt it important to tell as many people as possible how they dealt with trespassers. By openly boasting about the shooting, they were clearly issuing a warning to anyone who might be foolish enough to follow their tracks next time.

Walz and Weiser soon headed back to their blood-stained glory-hole and, once again, their excursion ended in violence.

They were much more cautious now. When their supplies began to dwindle, they decided that only one of them would go out for provisions while the other stayed behind to guard the diggings. A coin toss selected Walz to saddle up and lead the mules down the canyon. He was gone for several days. When he returned, he came upon a horrifying scene.

His partner was pinned to the ground by an arrow through his chest. The ashes of the campfire were still smoldering —a clear sign that the atrocity had been committed a very short time ago. Walz instantly swung his horse around and galloped away as fast as he could. But poor old Weiser was not yet dead. He regained consciousness, somehow managed to get to his feet, and lurched out of the mountains. In the desert beyond, he was picked up by the Pimas who took him to a ranch north of Florence. The rancher's wife, Mrs. Walker, did her best to treat his badly infected wound, but it was too late. Jacob Weiser died within a few days.

Jacob Walz now became a total loner. He continued to make solitary trips to his secret mine. Rumors floated —all unproven— that he killed several men who tried to follow him. He came out of the mountains for the last time in 1884, carrying only two small sacks of gold which sold for a mere $50. The Dutchman was 74 years old now, still tough but getting slow and feeble. It was time to retire.

He had set himself up pretty well for his final years. Unlike many other men who had struck it rich during that freewheeling era, Walz was not an ostentatious man. He had no desire to live in a mansion nor ride around in a fancy carriage. He had purchased a full section of raw land above the northern bank of the Salt River, just south of the original Phoenix townsite. There he built a modest adobe home and planted an orchard. He raised hogs and chickens, and, according to some historians, spent his nights in a typical Germanic way: drinking beer.

If so, he usually drank alone. He was reclusive, a bachelor who had never shared any part of his life with a woman. It was ironic, then, that his last and possibly truest friend was female, a rather mysterious woman half his age and of a different race.

Julia Thomas was a mulatto, a widow who ran a bakery and confectionery in what was then downtown Phoenix. She probably became acquainted with Walz because he sold eggs which she needed for her baking. Perhaps they were drawn together by a bond of loneliness. For whatever reason, Thomas grew very fond of the old man and visited him often. Finally, as Walz's health declined, she became his nurse.

She had no formal medical training and relied instead on her extensive knowledge of mystic healing. Her magic must have been strong, for Jacob Walz lived to the ripe old age of 81. He might have lived even longer had it not been for a cataclysmic "act of God" in 1891.

In February of that year, a monstrous flash flood roared down the Salt River, flooding across farmlands in the valley. Walz fled from his house in his long night shirt and was swept away by the deluge. He was found two days later, perched like a drenched ghost on the branch of a fruit tree. He was in shock and almost dead from hypothermia. His home, pigs, chickens, and whatever gold he had allegedly buried beneath his hearth, had all disappeared in the river's furious rampage.

Julia Thomas took the old man into her own home, but there was little she could do for him. He contracted pneumonia. They both knew the bed he was lying in was his death bed. In his final hours, he asked for paper and pen. With a trembling hand, he drew a map and gave it to Julia. Then, according to the *Phoenix Daily*, "he died with a blessing for her on his lips."

Thomas attended Jacob Walz's funeral but when she returned home, she found it had been ransacked in her absence. Although her possessions were strewn all over the floor, there was only one thing missing —the map, which she had carefully tucked away in a dresser drawer. Needless to say, Julia Thomas was outraged. The old prospector had bequeathed his mine to her and, map or no map, nobody was going to get to it ahead of her. She felt she had a pretty good memory of the map, and believed her mystic powers would do the rest.

With the help of two male friends, Thomas became the first woman to search for what would forever be called The Lost Dutchman Mine. She and her companions had no trouble locating the Weaver's Needle and a waterhole to the northwest but, from there on nothing on the ground looked like the squiggly lines on Walz's crudely drawn map.

Each night, she would sit before the campfire, toss colored powders into the flames and watch the dancing images that appeared. They revealed nothing. The mountain refused to give up its secrets. Julia

Thomas made a crestfallen return to Phoenix within a fortnight. She never went back for a second try. Perhaps the one thing the flames told her was to stay away.

Now it was time for some comic-relief in this ongoing drama, time for an utterly preposterous character to step into the spotlight and strike a melodramatic pose. James Addison Reavis had written his own script, which, though it was only a sub-plot in the Lost Dutchman mystery, gave the people of Arizona a villain they could boo and hiss for many years.

Reavis was originally a streetcar conductor in St. Louis, Missouri. The commuters from whom he collected fares would probably have laughed out loud had they known this cap-tipping, Chaplinesque character would someday proclaim himself the "Baron of Arizona."

Like so many others, Reavis drifted out West in the 1870s hoping to get rich on the frontier. He worked at a variety of low-wage jobs, getting nowhere, until he realized he had a talent few frontiersmen possessed: penmanship. Reavis was very adept at copying the signatures of other men. Soon he was making a comfortable living forging false mining claims and selling them to unsuspecting newcomers from back East.

Naturally, his new occupation required him to travel a bit. In the course of his wanderings, he chanced to met a prominent Phoenix shopkeeper named Miguel L. Peralta.

"I have heard of you," Reavis told Peralta in a voice filled with admiration. "Indeed, all Arizona knows of the Peraltas. Your family once owned all the land from Phoenix to the headwaters of the Salt and Gila Rivers."

"Once that was true," Peralta acknowledged. "But

we could not prove it was ours. The royal documents were lost a hundred years ago. So the land was taken from us, sold, given out as homesteads, handed over to the railroad."

Reavis shook his head sadly and placed a sympathetic hand on Peralta's shoulder. "You have been done a great injustice, my friend. And injustice cannot be tolerated, not by righteous men such as we. I will make you a proposal: I will go in search of these lost documents, and when I find them, you and I as partners will reclaim this purloined kingdom." "Why not?" Peralta replied. "What have I got to lose?" Several years would pass before he would answer his own question.

After the bargain was struck, Reavis disappeared for a few months. Then one day, he burst through the doors of the M.L. Peralta store waving a thick sheaf of elegant-looking papers. "I have succeeded beyond my wildest expectations!" he cried. "I have been to the National Archives in Mexico City, and there I found all the proof we need."

Reavis spread the documents across Peralta's counter. "The grant is even larger than we thought... nearly 12 million acres. And look at this: you, sir, are a direct descendant of a Spanish Grandee, an Ensign of the Royal House. How I wish I could claim such lineage! I suppose I will have to choose a title of my own. How does 'the Baron of Arizona' strike you? It has a nice ring, don't you think?"

Reavis paused in his oration and almost as an afterthought said, "Oh, by the way, I will need a little money, just a small sum for legal fees, the proper attire to wear in the courtroom, that sort of thing."

And Miguel Peralta rang open his cash register.

The self-proclaimed baron wasted no time in pursuing his case. He began filing quit-claim suits against the landowners, ranchers and miners of the Salt River valley, winning a surprising number of them. To confirm himself as one of the Peralta heirs, he courted and wed one of Miguel L. Peralta's daughters, and changed his name to Peraltareavis. For a time, it looked like he actually was going to establish his barony.

Peraltareavis became the most hated man in Arizona. The territorial newspapers openly editorialized that this "beak-nosed baron" could best be dealt with by a lynching party. But, ironically enough, the baron brought about his own downfall. In 1895 he audaciously sued the United States government for the return of the federal lands within his kingdom. These lands, by no coincidence, included the Superstition Mountains and the fabled Lost Dutchman Mine.

But this time the baron had gone too far. When *Peraltareavis vs the United States of America* came to trial, the government put enough paleographers, graphologists and linguists on the stand to prove Reavis' historical documents should be consigned to the nearest outhouse. They pointed out that the paper was fairly new, had been written on by steel pen nibs, and numerous Spanish words had been misspelled. Reavis' case was thrown out of court. He was indicted, tried and convicted for fraud in 1895.

Though his sentence was ten years, he served only two. He might have been better off had he stayed in prison since he spent the rest of his life roaming the frontier, a pathetic, threadbare old man still muttering about new schemes and great empires. He died November 20, 1914 at the age of 71, and was buried in a pauper's grave in Denver.

Miguel L. Peralta came to an even sadder end. Though he was not indicted in the scandal, he was financially ruined by it. His daughter, Lola, told the *Ari-*

zona Star, "That Reavis took and took and took from my father. Lands and houses, all were gone. Always grabbing, until my father had nothing left from his taking."

On November 5, 1897, Peralta went to the lonely room that now served as his home, spread a piece of paper on the table, and wrote: "I had money. I lost it. Goodbye." He weighted the paper down with his last silver dollar, pressed a pistol to his head and pulled the trigger.

That pistol shot should have brought down the curtain on this tragic drama, but it was not to be. Still more death scenes had to be acted out on the stage of the Superstitions. The cursed mountain range continued to lure victims well into the 20th century. The one who is best remembered was Adolph Ruth, a former postal clerk from Washington, D.C.

Ruth had been a "lost treasure buff" almost all his life. He had read everything he could find about the Lost Dutchman Mine, but it was not until his retirement in 1931 that he had a chance to go look for it.

Upon his arrival in Arizona in June of that year, Ruth paid a couple of wranglers to take him and a load of provisions to the Willow Spring waterhole several miles northwest of the Weaver's Needle. When the cowboys returned a few weeks later to replenish the old gent's supplies, they found his campsite empty. His tent was still set up and his gear was intact. But ominously, his boots were standing beside his bedroll. A search was initiated, and although the surrounding area was thoroughly combed by men, dogs and airplanes, it was not until December that the skull of Adolph Ruth was finally discovered.

It was lying on a ledge high up in West Boulder Canyon, over five miles from his campsite. The forehead of this well-bleached cranium had a neat, round hole in it which, according to those who first peered through it, appeared to have been "inflicted by a bullet." Within a few weeks, the rest of Ruth's skeleton was located in a dense tangle of brush almost a full mile from the skull.

Bits and pieces of the former postal clerk were taken to Phoenix to be examined by a team of doctors. Their conclusion: Ruth died of thirst and was then chewed up by coyotes or javelinas. This explanation did not satisfy everyone; a lot of folks continued to believe the old man had been murdered by someone who thought he had a treasure map.

The Ruth case got more publicity, but there were many more, equally mysterious and oddly similar, fatalities in the Superstitions during the 20th century. Most people who died in these hazardous mountains in recent times simply tripped and fell off cliffs or were shot by careless hunters. A disturbing number of people have deliberately chosen the Superstitions as an appropriate place to take their own lives, invariably with handguns.

But it is the other deaths, the ones that will forever remain unexplained, that are the most haunting and downright spooky. It seemed like the same scene was being played out over and over.

In 1949, James A. Cravey of Phoenix hired a helicopter pilot to fly him into the heart of the mountain range and drop him off with provisions for eight days. He planned to hike back out, but instead he vanished. Eight months later, a pair of horse riders from a dude ranch stumbled upon Cravey's headless skeleton near Bluff Springs, east of the Weaver's Needle. His skull was later pulled out of a hackberry thicket, 30 feet from the body.

In October, 1960, a group of hikers came across

the skeleton of Franz Harrer, an exchange student from Austria. It took four more days to find Harrer's skull; as usual, it was perforated by a distinct hole in the forehead. The bones of William Harvey of San Francisco turned up a couple of weeks later, followed by the discovery of the remains of a Salt Lake resident, Hilmer Bohen, three months after that. During the same year, a seasoned prospector named Jay Clap disappeared on one of his frequent trips into the Superstitions. In March, 1964, his skeleton was finally recovered, but his skull is still out there somewhere.

Over the years, a lot of people have argued about the probable cause of these hapless, headless victims. Were they murdered, all in the same way? Or were they simply victims of a terribly cruel environment? Had they been shot and beheaded, or had they died of dehydration and had their bones picked clean by scavengers? After all, a javelina's tooth is about the same size as a small calibre bullet. One explanation seems just as plausible as the other.

Maybe that's what makes the Lost Dutch Mine and the curse of the Superstitions so eternally fascinating. No two people will ever completely agree on exactly what did or did not happen during that incredible century and a half of searching. No one will ever know just what was really found or how much more remains lost. Nor can it be accurately determined how much blood was actually spilled.

The Pimas may have been right in their belief that anyone who offends these mountains will be punished by them. When one walks the trails of the Superstitions today, it is easy to believe there really is a strange power here, something that can be sensed but cannot be seen or defined... something that warns and lures at the same time.

If so, it is very likely that the legendary treasure of the Superstition Mountains will always remain just out of reach.

How To Get to the Weaver's Needle

From the town of Apache Junction, located 25 miles east of Phoenix, take Highway 88 (The Apache Trail) northeast for five miles to the Lost Dutchman State Park. Though only a corner of the mountain is visible from the park, it is an awesome sight, especially at sunset.

The campground has 35 undeveloped sites suitable for tents or self-contained RVs. Several hiking trails, ranging from easy to strenuous, form loops beyond the park boundary, allowing you to venture into the Superstition Mountains, now a U.S. Forest Service wilderness area. Drinking water is available in the campground, so don't forget to take along plenty when you hike. Maximum summer temperatures are often over 100 degrees, but the October-to-April period is usually quite pleasant.

Bibliography - Chapter 2

Arnold, Oren. **Superstitions' Gold.** San Antonio. Naylor Company, 1974.

Bagwell, Mary L. *Desert* magazine. Palm Desert, California. January 1954.

Blair, Robert. **Tales of the Superstitions.** Tempe, Arizona, Arizona Historical Foundation. 1975.

Gentry, Curt. **The Killer Mountains: A Search for the Legendary Lost Dutchman Mine.** New York. Ballentine Books. 1968.

Jennings, Gary. **The Treasure of the Supersti-**

tion Mountains. New York. W.W. Norton & Company. 1973.

Mitchell, John. **Lost Mines of the Great Southwest.** Glorieta, New Mexico. 1966.

3

Padre Kino and the
Blue Maiden from the Sky

"I undertake this journey in the name of the Most
Holy Trinity, the Most Holy Mary and all the blessed
souls in Purgatory."

The hand over the diary paused momentarily,
then continued to write. "Although for some months I
have had very poor health and even yet find myself
with little strength, I prepared the necessary pack animals and food and some small gifts for the natives.

With evangelical zeal, I shall be hoping against hope that much Honor and Glory will be achieved for the Two Majesties — God and King. Amen."

Father Eusebio Francisco Kino lay down his quill pen, closed his diary and blew out his candle. He stepped through the doorway of the hilltop mission of Nuestra Señora de los Dolores and stood beneath the stars. In the darkness beyond Dolores lay a vast, unexplored land, a great, sprawling expanse of merciless desert, life-giving rivers and range after range of unnamed mountains. It was a land upon which no Catholic priest had ever set foot; no one as yet had carried the cross of Christianity into this remote, hitherto ignored part of New Spain.

Kino was standing on the very rim of Christendom, waiting for dawn, at which time he and his entourage would go forth toward a blank space on the map called Pimaria Alta in 1697. Padre Kino was no stranger to rigorous travel; he was, in fact, one of the most widely traveled men of his time. Born in Italy in 1645, educated as a Jesuit in Germany, he was sent to Mexico City as a missionary in 1680. In the following year, he traveled to the port of Nio and sailed with the expedition of Admiral Isidro de Atondo y Antillon to Baja California.

From there, it was back to northern Mexico, where during the next 16 years, Kino built scores of missions, converted thousands of Indians and helped them establish cattle ranches. The black-robed padre's explorations took him all the way to the confluence of the Colorado and Gila Rivers in what is now Arizona. He was an inexhaustible man who, it is said, could ride 30 to 40 miles in a day and then sit up half the night reading.

He would definitely need that kind of stamina

when he headed north from his comfortable hearth in Dolores. But, as always, Kino was eager to be under way, to do as he had done so many times before: to be the first to bring the word of God to a heathen people who were otherwise doomed to an afterlife in Purgatory.

The first rays of dawn had scarcely reached the hilltop when Padre Kino, several other priests, Pima Indian converts, muleteers and a handful of government officials set off on their mission. During the first few days, they followed the peaceful course of the Rio Cocospara and rested at night in the mud-brick missions along their route —Remedios, Tumacacori and finally San Xavier del Bac, all products of the restless priest's zeal.

But north of San Xavier del Bac the true wilderness lay, extending all the way from present day Tucson to the Sacaton Mountains above Casas Grandes and east to the San Pedro Valley. Within this 2,800 mile area were more than two dozen Pima villages. Kino began visiting them to bring the word of Christ.

Although the Pima Indians already had a fine religion of their own, they were, according to the padre's diary, quite receptive to the new faith he offered. Each night, he praised God as he carefully recorded the numbers of baptisms he and the other priests had performed during the day. Kino's procession moved steadily north until it reached the most remote villages —where a curious thing happened.

As the dusty caravan approached a village in the Gila Valley, the people came streaming out of their homes to welcome the missionaries. The Indians were dressed ceremoniously with tall feathers in their headbands and brightly colored paint on their faces. They thronged around Kino, laughing and smiling as they helped him down from his horse. The flustered padre recovered his dignity, raised his arms and began to speak of the God whose only son had died on the cross.

"*Hau`u, mach s'ta machma,*" the Indians shouted. "Yes, we know of this. *Gahgi!* Look! We, too, wear crosses just as you do." The Jesuits stared in amazement as the villagers lifted the hand-carved wooden crucifixes that dangled from their necks.

Kino was stunned. "How can this be?" he must have asked. "We are the first to carry the cross of Christianity into this land."

"No," the Pima answered. "There was some one before you, a woman who came from the sky where your God lives." Padre Kino gathered his robes around his knees, sat down and, for a change, listened to the Indians.

"None of us ever saw her," the Pimas told him. "It was many years ago. But the *huhugam* —the elders— told us about her. They said they looked up one day, and she was standing on top of a hill. At first, she was hard to see, for her robes blended with the color of the sky. Soon, she walked down to the village carrying two crossed pieces of wood upon which the figure of a dead man was suspended. The people shrank away from this ghastly image, but the strange woman spoke to them in a gentle, reassuring voice, and their fears vanished."

Through gestures and words that were difficult to understand, the *S-kohmagi U'uwi* —the Blue Maiden— explained that the man on the cross was no longer dead. He had risen and gone to a place called Heaven, high above the tallest mountain. All who believed in Him would join Him there some day, she said, for He loved everyone who lived on the earth which His Father had created. After she had finished speaking, she clutched the wooden cross to her breast, returned to the hill top and faded again into the sky.

Surely anyone who witnessed such an astonishing event would have been awestruck, but for the Pimas, this visitation rocked the very foundations of their own religious beliefs. Like other Southwestern Indians, they knew the Gods lived in the Underworld, not above the clouds.

Pima cosmology taught that creation began when darkness rubbed against water, causing *Wehpeg Mahsikam* —First Born— to emerge. The wind carried this child across the black, empty void. At each place He stopped, He brought forth living things: first algae, then insects, plants, animals, and finally, people. No one was happy living in darkness, so First Born made a sun come up in the sky to warm the people by day, and He created a moon and a million stars to comfort them at night.

The Pimas knew all of this had actually happened, but, after listening to the mysterious Blue Maiden, they began to wonder if there was more to the story. Could there be other gods in the universe besides their own? They wanted to learn more, so when the *S-kohmagi U'uwi* made her second appearance, she drew a sizable crowd. By now, the Pima medicine men —*mamakai*— were growing very jealous. After the Blue Maiden disappeared again, they belittled her message. "How could her God live in the sky?" they scoffed. "Where would He sit?" When the shimmering woman returned for the third time, the *mamakais'* anger boiled over, and they shot her full of arrows.

The Blue Maiden fell to the ground, apparently dead. But moments later, she rose, shed the arrows and levitated into the sky, just as the man on the cross had done. After that, the Pimas started carving crosses of their own.

Padre Kino was not sure what to make of these strange tales, but he dutifully recorded them in his diary before traveling on to the next village. Here, he was approached by a man who asked him if he had any blue cloth. When Kino asked him why, the man said he wished to give some to his aged grandmother. She was very fond of that color, he said, for when she was just a child, she had frequently been visited by a beautiful woman dressed in blue garments. Now that she was old and knew her remaining days were limited, she wished to have her shroud made of blue cloth.

Padre Kino was totally perplexed; in all his travels, he had never encountered anything this inexplicable. Yet, when he moved on east to the settlements along the Rio San Pedro, he heard the same story over and over: during a time long past, a Blue Maiden had come down from the sky and preached to the Desert People.

"These Indians who live so far away from each other confirm this tale, so we must wonder if it is true," Kino told the other Jesuits. "Perhaps, at some later day, further inquiries and investigations should be made."

But further investigations, had they been conducted in Pimaria Alta, would not have solved the mystery. The solution to this enigma could only be found in a very distant place —in a small village thousands of miles from the dusty province of New Spain.

This village was called Agreda. It was located in the northern sector of Old Castile in Spain where, in 1635, a very remarkable nun who called herself María de Jesús de Agreda wrote her autobiography. Though she was only 33 at the time, she already had an extraordinary life to write about.

She had been born María Coronel on April 2, 1602. At the age of 17, she entered the convent in Agreda where the colors of the nuns' habits were blue and grey. María had only been in the convent for two years when amazing things began happening to her.

In 1621, she reported experiencing a fantastic vision. She claimed the Lord came to her, showed her the whole world, and told her of His concern for the multitudes of non-Christians inhabiting it. Shortly after that, she went into a trance and found herself standing on a hill top above a primitive village in a far-away land. She drifted down from the hill and spoke to the bronze-skinned people who gathered around her. A few hours later, she awoke in her own bed in Agreda.

Her trances re-occurred at regular intervals. Before long, she had made many miraculous visitations to the farthest reaches of New Spain. Sometimes, she would find herself standing on the bank of a river, with the Indians all waiting on the other side. This posed no problem since she could simply rise and float above the water until she stepped down on the opposite shore. María wrote that once some of the Indians attempted to kill her with their bows and arrows, but most of the time the people were very friendly and respectful. Over a period of ten years, 1621-31, she reported making many conversions among the Indians of New Spain.

That ten-year period was an important decade in her life in other ways as well. In 1627, when she was only 25, she was elected *presidente* of the Agreda convent where she ruled for the next 24 years. She also took the name María de Jesús —the name by which she would eventually become both famous and controversial within the Catholic hierarchy of Spain.

When María de Jesús completed her autobiography, she presented it to the local Franciscan authorities along with a request that it be published. The Franciscans read the manuscript carefully, then shook their heads and handed it back to her.

"It is best if no one ever sees this," they cautioned. "Who will believe you? It will be said that you were dreaming, or, at worst, you will be accused of deliberately fabricating miracles. It is our decision that you must burn this book along with any other manuscripts you may have written."

María de Jesús dutifully obeyed her superiors. The book was burned; it seemed the matter had been laid to rest. Fifteen years went by before the mystic nun's incredible story resurfaced.

In 1650, a friar named Ximenez Samaniego was thumbing through the church's archives in Agreda when he chanced upon a document which mentioned the Franciscan's suppression of the writings of María de Jesús. Curious, Samaniego spoke with her. Once he had heard her stories, he became a firm believer; he decided that since she was not allowed to write about her own life, he would do it for her.

Samaniego worked on María's biography for several years but it was still unfinished at the time of her death in 1666. The ponderous manuscript was finally completed and published in Madrid in 1669. As the Franciscans had predicted years before, church officials quickly polarized over the validity of the alleged miracles. "Where is the proof?" the skeptics demanded. "María de Jesús lived all of her life in the village of Agreda. Why should anyone believe she made celestial visits to the New World?"

"The Lord will verify His work in His own good time," María's defenders replied. "Until then, we must accept these miracles on faith."

The controversy was finally resolved in 1699 when Padre Kino's reports reached Mexico City and were relayed to Spain. Now, few could deny that this holy woman had somehow traveled extensively in the outer regions of Pimaria Alta more than 70 years ahead of the Kino expedition. The debate shifted to a theological discussion of her means of passage. Did she travel in body or in spirit only? Since she was struck by arrows during one of her appearances, it hardly seemed possible she was there physically.

María de Jesús had told Samaniego that she eventually concluded that her spirit was united with that of an angel, thus enabling her to be transmitted instantaneously. But regardless of how she channeled herself, the Spanish church officials were sufficiently impressed to attempt to have her beatified in the early 1700s. The Jesuits managed to block these efforts, however, because the nun's accomplishments tended to overshadow their own considerable achievements in New World soul-saving.

When Padre Eusebio Francisco Kino passed away in 1711, his bones were interred in California. His odysseys across the Southwest made him a legend in his own time. The missions he established —many of which still stand today— assure him a permanent place in history.

María de Jesús de Agreda built no missions; she left no mark upon the land she visited so many times. She sailed no seas, nor rode at the head of any great caravans. Nonetheless, she, like Kino, was one of the great travelers of her day. The maiden in blue never met the padre in black, at least not in this world. But, if they chanced to meet in the afterlife in which they both so fervently believed, what wondrous stories they must have shared.

How to Get to María de Jesús' Pimaria Alta Missions

Padre Eusebio Francisco Kino established 50 missions in Sonora, Mexico and Arizona. Nearly all of these ancient places of worship have long since crumbled back into the soil. But two of the Arizona missions have been preserved as national monuments.

San Jose de Tumacacori is located 18 miles north of Nogales along Highway 89. It started as a simple shelter in 1691, and became a major mission in 1773. After it was abandoned in the 1840s, it fell into ruin and was not restored and stabilized until after it gained status as a national monument in 1908.

San Xavier del Bac is located south of Tucson, between Interstate 19 and Highway 89. The original mission was consecrated in 1797 and was later replaced by the glistening white combination of Byzantine, Moorish and Spanish architecture that is carefully preserved today.

Bibliography - Chapter 3

Bakker, Elna and Lillard, Richard G. **The Great Southwest.** New York. Weathervane Books, 1962.

Bolton, Herbert Eugene. **Rim of Christendom.** Tucson. The University of Arizona Press. 1984.

Paylore, Patricia P. **Kino: A Commemoration.** Tucson. Arizona Pioneers' Historical Society. 1961.

Saxton, Dean and Lucille. **Legends and Lore of the Papago and Pima Indians.** Tucson. The University of Arizona Press. 1973.

Smith, Fay Jackson, Kessell, John L. and Kox, Francis J. **Father Kino in Arizona.** Phoenix. Arizona

Historical Foundation. 1966.

    Wagner, Henry R. **The Spanish Southwest. 1542-1794.** Part II. New York. Arno Press. 1967.

4

Mysteries of the Hopis

Most creation myths begin in empty darkness.

The Christian Bible opens with a very short description of a formless earth covered with black water, a world devoid of firmament and life until a spirit named God brought forth light and living creatures by simply commanding them to appear. At the same time that the ancient authors of the Bible were struggling to explain the mysteries of genesis, the Indians of North America were also contemplating the inexplicability of creation. They, however, realized the origin of the world and the life that exists upon it and within it was such a complex and lengthy process that it could hardly have been accomplished by a single god in a single week.

Each Indian tribe in the Western Hemisphere, from the southern tropics to the Arctic north, can trace its ancestral roots back to primordial realms where multitudes of gods dwell. These are gods possessed of great powers, rich imaginations and hopeful dreams for the people they guided into the lands they created. All Native American religions are sublimely beautiful, but surely none is more fascinating than that of the Hopi people of Arizona.

According to Hopi cosmogony, there was only one god at the beginning of time. He was Tawa, the Sun Spirit, and He was surrounded by endless, empty space. Yet, in His mind, He envisioned an entire world which He believed He could create by assembling the various elements drifting in the great void around Him. The world Tawa dreamed of would be a perfect one, inhabited by people and animals living in complete harmony. But He knew He could not do it alone, so He called forth Spider Woman to assist Him.

When Spider Woman came into being, she looked about, blinking in the dim, purple light, and asked the two most important questions that any inhabitant of any world can ask: "Who am I? And why am I here?"

"You are Spider Woman," Tawa answered. "You are here to help me make a world. I will gather in the substance you will need." Tawa drew all the elements together to form earth and water. Spider Woman, using her saliva, began molding clay into many shapes. When she sang to them, they came to life. Soon, the newly-born world was covered with plants, animals and finally people. It was a good world, but it was far from perfect.

Evil forces began to creep in, tempting and corrupting the people. First came The Talker, in the form of a mockingbird. He sowed dissension wherever he went. People and animals were not meant to live together, he preached. Nor should people of different skin colors and languages associate peacefully.

Next came Kato'ya, the Big Headed Snake. His mesmerizing gaze and his beguiling tongue lured even more people away from their pristine wisdom. Before long, animals were fleeing from humans, and tribal warfare was breaking out across the land.

Tawa was terribly displeased. He summoned all the deities (by this time were were many) and He said, "I am going to destroy this world and build another." He ordered Spider Woman to guide the good people deep into the kiva of the ants. Then, He incinerated the earth. Volcanoes erupted, lava flowed, the sky became an inferno.

When the earth cooled at last, the people emerged into a new world. This second world was larger than the first and even more bountiful... so bountiful, in fact, that the people quickly became greedy and materialistic. They began accumulating wealth, hoarding and stealing, fighting among themselves more than ever before. So once again, Tawa sent the people who were still righteous into the Underworld of the ants, and then reluctantly destroyed His second world by encasing it in ice.

When the ice finally melted, the people emerged into their third world. This world was the finest they had seen so far; it was lush, very fertile, and had plenty of fresh water. But it was still not cleansed of evil. Somehow, the evil spirits always managed to survive and come back stronger than ever. Powerful sorcerers were walking and flying across the land. They tricked the people with false doctrines, convinced them to be lazy and promiscuous, jealous and hateful, and they brought sickness and death to anyone who opposed them.

The people who still remained true to Tawa's

original plan of creation were shocked and frightened. They knew they would have to leave this unholy world and travel upward again. But this time they would also have to find a way to keep the evil ones from following them. Some of the more observant had noticed a hole in the the sky —a *sipa'puni*— high above them. They realized that if they could reach the *sipa'puni* they could enter their fourth and final world.

The good people planted a corn stalk and convinced Spider Woman to teach them the songs needed to make it grow. As the peoples' voices rose, so did the stalk; it grew like no other corn stalk had ever grown, taller and taller until it passed through the *sipa'puni*. Now Spider Woman gave the people very careful instructions: "Your journey to the Upper World will be long and difficult," she said. "Carry no possessions, for you will need both hands for climbing. Be sure that none who have performed wicked deeds follow you. I will go first and will be there to welcome you and tell you more about who you are about to become."

With that, Spider Woman gracefully ascended the corn stalk, the Twin Warrior Boys, Pokanhoya and Polongahoya climbing after her. The people followed and soon the entire stalk was completely covered with an upwardly moving mass of human beings. When the first group emerged from the *sipa'puni*, Spider Woman greeted them, "You shall be Hopis and speak the Hopi language."

To the next group, she said, "You shall be Navajos and speak the Navajo language."

She assigned all the people to specific tribes and gave each a special language —Apache, Pima, Zuni, Ute and many others. The last to emerge were a people with very pale skins; to them, Spider Woman said, "You will be the *Bahannas* —the White People— and you will speak many languages. You will travel far from this place but someday you will return."

By now, the evil creatures had discovered the corn stalk. They swarmed around the roots, clutching at the leaves, pulling themselves up. The Twin Warrior Boys knelt beside the plant, grasped it, shook it vigorously, and sent the wicked ones tumbling down like a great shower of grain. Then the Twins gave the stalk a mighty tug to pull its roots from the ground. They dropped it back into the Lower World. Spider Woman covered the *sipa'puni* with water to make it resemble an ordinary pond. Finally the people breathed a great collective sigh of relief. They were safe in their new world. All evil had been left behind... or so they thought.

Only a few days had passed before the son of the *Kikmongwi* —the Hopi chief— suddenly grew violently ill and died. Immediately the people came to the chilling realization that, in spite of all their precautions, there was a sorcerer in their midst. Somehow, at least one creature from the dark side of life had managed to slip through undetected during the emergence. The people looked distrustfully at one another, but they could not determine who among them was the one with the evil heart.

The new *kikmongwi* made a ball out of corn meal and threw it into the air above the crowd. It fell on the head of a young woman, the very last one who had climbed through the *sipa'puni.* "So," the *kikmongwi* said, "you are the one."

The young woman's eyes now began to glow and her innocent smile curved into a thin, subtle sneer. "Yes, I am a sorceress," she admitted. "But there is nothing you can do about it now. You cannot kill me, nor can you send me back to the Lower

World. I am here to stay."

The *kikmongwi* paced back and forth with this hands clasped behind his back. Finally, he whirled around and pointed his finger at the sorceress. "Your presence has already contaminated our new world," he snapped. "You brought evil to us, and evil always spreads. We now know that we will always have to struggle against wickedness no matter where we live. But, when we travel on in search of the center of this world, you will not go with us. You are forbidden to travel with the Hopi people."

The sorceress covered her face with her hands and peeked coyly from between her fingers. In a voice as sweet and shy as a child's, she asked, "What will become of me?"

Now the *Bahannas* spoke up. "She can come with us," they said. "We are not afraid of her. And, perhaps, her powers will be useful to us."

And so the sorceress went with the *Bahannas*, together travelling far, far away. The Hopis, too, set forth on epic journeys. The tribe divided itself into clans, each heading off in a different direction. Guided by falling stars, fickle winds and drifting clouds, they wandered for years seeking the place that was meant to be their eternal homeland. At last, they all converged in the harsh, wind-scoured rock mesas of northeastern Arizona. Here they built their villages, planted crops and fruit trees and perfected their culture.

The story of the Hopi's Emergence and their subsequent Great Migration is a wonderful tale which, until fairly recently, was passed down through the ages only as oral history. Although the story was told many times by many generations, it had only been written down in one way. Long before anthropologists with their notebooks came to the land of the Hopi, the entire

Hopi creation story was expressed by a single, very intricate symbol. Appropriately, that symbol is a maze.

It is usually called the *T'apu'at*, meaning Mother and Child, or simply Mother Earth. The symbol is a rectangle drawn with a single, continuous line which begins and ends within the maze itself. The line cuts back and forth, and up and down at sharp 90-degree angles, forming a complex pattern with an opening on one side. A short, straight line, which begins at the exact center of the maze, passes through the opening. This line symbolizes the path of Emergence —a spiritual umbilical cord originating in the great, cosmic womb of Mother Earth.

The *T'apu'at* has been carved in five places on a rock south of the village of Oraibi, and another appears on an inside wall in the Casa Grande ruin near Florence. The most intriguing thing about this distinctive symbol is that it is not unique to the Hopis. The same symbol has been found in many faraway places and is identical to the *T'apu'at* in every respect. This labyrinthian pattern has been discovered in ancient Quiche Mayan ruins, in Cuenca, Ecuador (territory of the Incas) —and in Britain, Scandinavia and in the Mediterranean region.

The original symbol is derived from the religious art of Knossos in Crete, and it appears on many old Cretan coins. It was also engraved on a wall in Pompeii, south of Naples. The Cretan interpretation of the maze symbol is, however, quite different from the Hopi version. Above the Pompeiian inscription, these words are carved into the stone: "The Labyrinth maze, here dwells the Minotaur."

It may be then, that the original drawings of the maze symbolize not a place of emergence, but a place of confinement —a depiction of the labyrinth built by the mythical Dædalus to imprison a dreaded beast. And strangely enough, petroglyphs of the half-man, half-bull Minotaur have been found at places in Texas where simplified versions of the maze were carved nearby.

Is this, perhaps, an indication that ancient visitors from the Mediterranean introduced the symbol into the New World, and that the Hopis learned to draw it from them?

Or does another theory apply? Some anthropologists believe the Hopis may have come to this country from across the Pacific, in boats rather than on foot, via the Bering Strait. These early voyagers might have been the founders of the Mayan civilization, and perhaps the Hopis branched off from them and migrated north. The full story of the Hopi's origin is unlikely ever to be completely known. The events which led them to develop such a rich and complex religion may well remain a mystery forever.

The Hopi religion served them well for countless generations. It brought not only beauty to their lives but enabled them to survive in a bleak and often hostile landscape. The Hopi's rainmaking powers are probably the best example of their remarkable ability to exercise a degree of control over their environment without damaging it in the process.

Very little rain falls on the land of the Hopis. Originally, the people relied primarily on the springs and water seeps at the bases of the cliffs below their villages. Orchards, corn fields and compact, terraced gardens were carefully tended to utilize every drop of water. Overall, this agricultural system worked well, but the springs needed to be replenished by rain. When the rains do not come, the whole system is endangered.

The Hopis realized from the start that communications between themselves and the water gods would have to be continuously and scrupulously maintained. It was well known that snakes are the messengers who convey prayers from the people on the land to the spirits who live below, since snakes constantly travel back and forth between both realms. Therefore ceremonies involving snakes are extremely important rituals.

Music can also be an effective means of communication. In fact, members of the Blue and Grey Flute Clans believe their flute ceremonies are even more powerful for rainmaking purposes than the ceremonies performed by the Snake Clan. Consequently, the two clans alternate their ceremonies every year to be doubly sure that the gods have been contacted.

The Flute Clans came to the Hopi lands at the end of the Great Migration. They were the last to arrive since they had traveled the farthest —they had gone all the way to the snow-capped arctic region before turning back. When at last they reached the Hopi village of Walpi, the Flute people climbed the narrow trail up the cliffs in a single file while their leader played a haunting melody on his flute.

The villagers sprinkled a line of corn meal across the path ahead of them, and when the newcomers halted at this barrier, the Walpi Snake priest asked them, "Who are you? And why are you here?"

"We are wanderers searching for a home," the Flute priest replied. "We are of Hopi blood, and our hearts are clean. On our backs, we carry the Flute altar, and we can cause dry springs to bubble with water and clouds to spill rain on parched fields."

The Snake priests brushed away the strip of corn meal, allowing the outsiders to enter the village. They led the Flute priests down into a kiva and watched skeptically as the strangers prepared to demonstrate their powers. The Flute priests dropped kernels of corn into the cracks between the rocks in the kiva floor. Then the priests of the Blue Flute Clan played their sky-blue flutes while the Grey Flute Clan priests blew softly through their storm-cloud colored flutes. A column of rain fell through the hatchway in the roof of the kiva.

All night, they played and sang their wondrous songs. By morning, sturdy green stalks of corn grew where the Flute priests had planted kernels into the soft earth. The Snake priests were greatly impressed. "You are welcome here," they said. "Your *kikmongwi* shall be one of our priests." And so, from that time on, the Flute and Snake Clans shared the responsibility of bringing summer rains to Hopi farm lands.

Ceremonies of both clans are held in August, but the preparations begin far in advance. During the year of the Flute Clan's ceremonies, medicine water must be mixed in winter and sprinkled with an eagle feather over the seeds which have been placed on the sacred altar. Later, feathered prayer sticks are blessed, smoked over, and placed in special locations around the village. The actual ceremony lasts 16 days, during which there is much praying in the kivas, a sand painting is produced and the Gone-Aways are honored.

On the final day, elaborate dances and foot races are held before small blue rings are tossed into the muddy Flute spring. Late in the day, the Flute priests enter a small cottonwood-branch shelter. Here, seated before a water jar symbolizing the original *sipa'puni*, they pray and make offerings of corn meal on the altar. After dark, a great chorus gathers in the plaza to sing until dawn.

Although the Flute ceremony is mystic and lovely, it always has been the Snake ceremony that has been most fascinating to outsiders. The sight of painted men dancing in a plaza with live rattlesnakes in their mouths invariably captivates, awes, and sometimes repulses the non-Indian visitors who come each year to watch. Early officials of the U.S. Bureau of Indian Affairs were so shocked by the snake dances that they sought, unsucessfully, to have them banned. This only showed how poorly they understood the Hopi's special relationship with nature.

While most people regard rattlesnakes as creatures to be avoided at all times, or to be killed as quickly as possible when encountered, the Hopis have long known that if these venemous reptiles are treated respectfully, they need not be feared. They know that if the rattlesnakes trust them, they can trust the rattlesnakes.

The Snake ceremony requires even more preparation than the Flute ritual. Not only must an altar be erected, a sand painting created, and prayer sticks carved, the clan members must search the desert in each of the four directions searching for the snakes' faint tracks in the sand. Following the nearly imperceptible traces, they must capture the snakes with their bare hands. It goes without saying that this is not a task for the faint-hearted.

Each snake hunter carries an empty water jar, a small sack of corn meal and two buzzard feathers tied together. When a snake is discovered it will instinctively coil, buzz and ready itself to strike. Rule number one in the Snake Clan is never pick up a coiled snake. A rattler only coils to strike when it does not know what is in the mind and heart of the tall, two-legged creature approaching it. A Hopi snake hunter's first and most important task is to convince the snake that the two of them are brothers.

The hunter kneels before the frightened, angry reptile and gently waves the buzzard feathers over its head. When the snake relaxes, it is quickly grasped behind the back of its head and lifted off the ground. If the snake thrashes and fights back, it is stroked and rubbed with spit and corn meal until it calms down and hangs like a piece of rope from its captor's hand. Now the snake can be dropped into a water jar and carried back to the village.

A four-day snake hunt can yield as many as 50 to 60 reptiles. Some are bullsnakes and racers, but most are diamondbacks and sidewinders. The snakes' fangs are never extracted nor are their sacs of venom emptied, since this is injurious and demeaning to these sacred serpents. Instead, a special herbal medicine called *chu'knga* is drunk by each snake handler. In the event that someone is bitten, this same medicine is immediately applied to the wound. Since an ounce of prevention is worth at least as much as a pound of cure, the best practice is to avoid being bitten in the first place.

Most people might try to protect themselves from the lightning-fast blur of a rattler's strike by staying as far out of reach as possible. The Hopis use exactly the opposite approach; they get as close to the snakes as they possibly can.

On the night following the gathering of the snakes, the members of the clan descend into their kiva at midnight. After everyone is settled cross-legged on the floor, the perforated buckskin tops of the water jars are untied and the snakes are released. The snake's new brothers sit perfectly still and sing soft, peaceful songs as 50 or more serpents slither cautiously around the underground room, exploring, listening and tasting the air with their flickering tongues. Soon, when they realize they are in a non-threatening atmosphere, they begin crawling over the singers' legs, curling up in the men's laps to enjoy the warmth of human bodies.

When dawn comes, all the snakes are asleep and can be gently picked up and placed back in the water jars to await their roles in the upcoming ceremony.

Meanwhile, in the kiva of the Antelope Clan, two wooden images have been placed on the altar. One represents Snake Maiden, the other Antelope Boy. Just at midnight, as the eighth day of the ritual is about to begin, the human counterparts of these two dieties are brought into the kiva. Snake Maiden is a young virgin who has been chosen for her role by the women of the Snake Clan. Her face is painted half black and half white, and her long hair has been combed loosely down the back of her white and red cape.

Antelope Boy's hair also hangs loose on his shoulders. He wears a white kirtle around his waist, while his face, arms and legs have been painted with zig-zagging streaks of ash-white clay. This young couple is to be symbolically married in a mystic union which renews the bond between these two great clans. Antelope Boy carries a snake and Snake Maiden wears a turquoise and shell necklace from the Antelope Clan.

The two of them sit side by side while the elders wash their hair with a soap made of yucca roots and twist the couple's hair together while it is still wet. In this way, their highest psychic levels are spiritually joined; the feminine aspect of the universal forces awakens the divine consciousness which is latent in males, fuses these dual natures and releases the energies which make it possible for the priests to communicate with their gods.

After the teenagers have been blessed by the

priests of both clans, Snake Maiden's mother takes the girl back home and Antelope Boy goes home with his father. Dawn is breaking by this time, so many people are standing on their rooftops, watching the horizon. At first there is nothing to see, but as the earth turns slowly to the east, distant figures are sighted running toward the village. The antelope race is under way.

This event is the next step in the complex process of bringing gods and humans together. Now that the mystic marriage has opened the lines of communication, a pathway must be created to lead the gods to the village. This is the purpose of this strenuous race. The Antelopes run barefoot from a sacred starting point four miles east of the village plaza. They carry corn stalks and squash vines, but run at break-neck speeds toward their destination. As the crowd on the rooftops cheers, the runners dash, panting and sweating, up the rocky trail to the mesa top. When they burst into the plaza, everyone swarms forward laughing and waving corn stalks in a merry greeting. While the arrival is being celebrated noisily, the winner of the race is handed a special prayer stick which he takes to his family's corn field. Now everything is ready for the most important day of all —the day of the Snake dancers.

The final ceremony begins early in the afternoon when the Wind Roarer strides into the plaza and whirls a great stick which simulates the sound of rolling thunder. This strange, booming noise is a reverberating call to the clouds, urging them to rise from their distant shrines. Then, abruptly, the thunder stops. In the sudden silence, the Wind Roarer sets the stick aside, lifts up his bow and fires an arrow into the sky. The arrow vanishes in an instant, falling somewhere in the desert.

From the Snake kiva comes the faint rattle of

turtle shells and the jingle of silver ornaments as, one by one, the Snake dancers climb the ladder from their underground chamber and step out into the hot sunshine. Each has been painted from the waist up with dark red clay embellished with white snake designs. The dancers file into the clearing which by now is completely encircled by scores of onlookers. Individually, they enter the cottonwood-branch bower where the snakes have been placed upon the sand.

The Snake chief goes in first and is handed a snake by one of the priests. He takes it in his mouth, grasping it firmly but gently at the halfway point of its body, and lifts the serpent's drooping tail with his left hand. At the same moment, he feels the hand of another dancer encircling his shoulder. This second dancer is referred to as a "hugger"; he will hug the snake carrier with his left arm while he strokes the weaving head of the serpent with the long, soothing feathers he holds in his right hand. Together, they will dance, along with the other dancers and huggers, in perfect coordination four times around the plaza.

The hugger's role is a vitally important one but sometimes it is quite unnecessary. Occasionally a snake will become so contented that it will press its head peacefully against the carrier's warm, bare chest. When the dance has ended, the snakes are returned to the gatherers who take them back to shrines in the desert. There they are blessed for the last time and told to go on their way, carrying the people's message to the gods.

Back in the village, a feast has been prepared for all who participated in the ceremony. Thin sheets of corn meal *piki* bread have been fried on hot, greased stones. Since this is a special occasion, a pinch of sacred ashes has been added to the batter. Around the village, mutton, sweet squash with toasted pumpkin seed sauce, cake and plenty of hot coffee are served liberally. Everyone dines well and enjoys the satisfaction of having successfully performed a very difficult ritual.

Most observers would agree the snake dance is an impressive ceremony —but does it work? Can the dances really bring rain?

Traditional Hopis are quite certain that the dances do, indeed, bring rain. The efficacy of the ceremony is also attested to by numerous outsiders as well. There are plenty of accounts in which long-delayed rains fell within a few days of the ceremonies. Other observers reported thunderheads rising while the Snake ceremony was in progress, with showers just as the dances ended.

Dama Langley, who lived for a time at the village of Mishongnovi, watched clouds boil up over the sacred San Francisco Peaks southwest of the reservation during a flute dance in 1948, and she witnessed the same phenomenon in 1953 at the conclusion of a snake dance.

Frank Waters, a leading authority on the Hopi, wrote about a snake ceremonial he attended in 1961. It had been a very dry year; corn was wilting in the fields. At four in the afternoon, when the snake dancers filed into the plaza, a sharp wind suddenly blasted them with sand and dust. Dark, blue-black storm clouds swept across the northern horizon, the air grew cold and the people drew their thin, cotton blankets over their heads as icy raindrops pelted them. The rain was sparse and ended quickly, but the elders were satisfied. The water gods were acknowledging their awareness of the ceremony and promised more rain to come.

The most spectacularly successful rain dance is

said to have occurred on an unremembered date sometime before the turn of the century. It was a year of severe drought. The Navajo reservation was especially dry. Faced with starvation, many Navajo families moved onto the greener Hopi lands, bringing their sheep and horses with them. When the Hopis ordered them to leave, the Navajo refused fearing they and all their livestock would die.

Hopi elders held a council and decided that even though it was the wrong season for a rain dance, a special ceremony must be held. Whether the dance was performed by the Flute Clan or the Snake Clan is uncertain. But it brought immediate results. Both reservations were drenched with rain, the waterholes were refilled, the range revived and the Navajos returned to their own homes.

There are times, of course, when neither flutes nor snakes can bring the gift of rain to the desert. The Hopis always know they are asking a lot of their gods. And they know that if they make just one mistake in their supplications, if a ceremony is improperly performed in any small way, they can expect a dry year.

In recent times, additional problems have arisen; the Hopi religion now has to contend with outside forces hardly imaginable by the ancestral Gone-Aways. In 1989, one of the oldest and most sacred snake-gathering areas was destroyed to make room for a road improvement project's construction yard. Many shrines were plowed away by the contractors' bulldozers.

The theft of religious artifacts from Hopi lands has also had a devastating impact on their way of life. During the past three decades, nearly two-thirds of all the tribe's irreplaceable sacred objects and antiquities have been stolen and sold in the international black market where Hopi masks and kachina dolls can bring up to $100,000 apiece in Santa Fe, New York, Berlin or Tokyo. Plunderers sometimes equipped with police scanners, backhoes and even helicopters have clandestinely entered the reservation to loot ancient ruins and graves. Even kivas and clan houses have been violated by thieves who, all too often, are helped by Hopi accomplices who no longer believe in the old ways.

These massive desecrations are destroying one of the most profound religions our nation has ever known. As Peter Welsh, chief curator of the Heard Museum in Phoenix, has explained it, "If this were happening to Catholics or Jews, there would be such an outcry."

Once a holy relic disappears, or a shrine is profaned, a vital part of the total mystic fabric is torn away. The worst desecration of all occurred in 1978 when the *tala'yumsi* —the sacred representation of Dawn Woman— was stolen from its shrine in Shungopavi. The *tala'yumsi* was from time immemorial the centerpeice of one of the Hopis' most important and secretive rites —the *wu'wuchim* ceremony. Made of cottonwood roots with small faces painted on the ends, the *tala'yumsi* has so much power that most members of the tribe did not dare to look at it. The ritual in which it was used was the most carefully guarded of all ceremonials.

During *wu'wuchim*, the roads into the village were closed by priests of the One Horn Clan, who drew four corn meal lines across the roads to seal out any evil spirits that might attempt to enter. Any person —evil or innocent— who dares to cross these lines would die within four years (any animal or bird that crossed the lines was found dead in the morning). Good spirits were allowed to enter a village if, after being asked, "Who are you?" they answered, "I am I."

These apparitions faded at once into the village's adobe walls and were present throughout the ceremony.

The rites of *wu'wuchim* had to be completely pure and untainted for this was the ceremony in which young men were initiated into a higher stage of spiritual awareness. The ceremony enabled them to take the first step upward toward the mystic level of the elders. *Wu'wuchim* was a winter ceremonial, conducted each year in November, the month of Hawk Moon, on a date determined by lunar observations. Much of the sixteen-day ceremony took place at night, deep in the smokey interior of the Two Horn Clan kiva. The ritual was so enigmatic it was seldom talked about by participants.

Today, a true *wu'wuchim* ritual can no longer be held due to the theft of the *tala'yumsi*, thus denying an entire generation of young Hopis access to their forefathers' ancient wisdom.

Will this venerated object ever be recovered and returned? The Federal Bureau of Investigation is still working on the case, but even though leads and clues have been followed all the way to West Germany, no breakthrough in this crime has occurred. The whereabouts of the *tala'yumsi* and other stolen artifacts remains a mystery.

Perhaps the greatest mystery of the Hopis is whether or not the Hopi lifeway will continue to survive now that the world around it has once again changed forever. The Twentieth Century has not always been kind to the Hopis. True, deep wells and irrigation have reduced the need for rain dances, and solar power projects are bringing light to places that were previously dark, but the price of progress has been high. Since the return of the *Bahannas*, the Hopis have seen their ancestral lands reduced, their religion disrespected and their special insights toward nature belittled.

Hopi prophesies tell of a time in the not-too-distant future when Tawa will again be forced to destroy His now-contaminated Fourth World. The time will come when a Blue Star kachina dancer will remove his mask in front of all errant and uninitiated Hopis signaling the end of this world and the beginning of a new life-cycle in a Fifth World.

One can fervently hope that no further destruction of worlds will be necessary, but as long as Tawa's original dream of a perfectly virtuous world where all creatures live in harmony remains unfulfilled —who can say?

How to Visit the Land of the Hopis

A driving tour of several Hopi villages can begin by driving west from the junction of Highways 77 and 264, 55 miles north of Holbrook. The highway follows the great sandstone rim that runs past the small settlements of Keams Canyon, Polacco, and First Mesa. Then, 28 miles from the junction, the road climbs the rimrock in a spectacular swoop. Two miles over the mesa's crest, Shungopavi appears on the left. Two miles further west, one finds the Hopi Cultural Center with its fine museum, gift shop, restaurant and motel. All along the route there are many galleries and shops displaying and selling exquisite Hopi arts and crafts.

Ten miles beyond the cultural center, the once-imposing, now-crumbling village of Old Oraibi comes into view, perched on its lonely mesa. The Hopi people welcome visitors as long as they show respect. No photography is allowed. When you walk around a Hopi village, confine yourself to the roads and streets only. Do not pick up or remove any object.

Bibliography - Chapter 4

Associated Press. June 28, 1990.

Courlander, Harold. **The Fourth World of the Hopis.** New York. Fawcett Publications, Inc. 1971.

Dallas Morning News. July 8, 1990.

Euler, Robert C. and Dobyns, Henry F. **The Hopi People.** Phoenix. Indian Tribal Series. 1971.

Langley, Dama. *Desert* magazine. Palm Desert, California. August, 1950.

O'Kane, Walter Collins. **The Hopis: Portrait of a Desert People.** Norman, Oklahoma. Univeristy of Oklahoma Press. 1953.

O'Kane, Walter Collins. **Sun in the Sky.** Norman, Oklahoma. University of Oklahoma Press. 1950.

Simer, Myrtle Mae. *Desert* magazine. Palm Desert, California. July, 1949, August, 1954.

Waters, Frank. **Book of the Hopi.** New York. Viking Press, Inc. 1963.

5

Sojourns Through
The Evil Way

Most people will never see a ghost, let alone have to defend against one. Occasionally, an unsuspecting person may get a sudden, fleeting glimpse of something emerged from the shadowy realms of the supernatural, but generally, face-to-face encounters with earthbound spirits are fortuitously rare.

Other people live constantly in the presence of ghosts; they know that spirits can arise at any moment, during any time of night, to frighten them, threaten them —or even kill them. The Native Americans of Arizona, as elsewhere, have always been aware that they are forever surrounded by menacing figures from the world of the dead. The Navajos, the Apaches, Pimas and Maricopas, as well as their prehistoric ancestors, the Hohokams, have all had to find ways to protect themselves from this never-ending peril.

The Navajos learned during the earliest of times that the only people who rest peacefully after death are those who die of old age, or die at birth. All others become ghosts. Once they leave their bodies, the ghosts are guided into the subterranean Afterworld by the spirits of their relatives and, though the Afterworld is quite similar to the Surfaceworld, its inhabitants are not always happy there.

Sometimes they are deeply disturbed because their burial ceremony was conducted improperly, or their most meaningful possessions were not interred with them. For reasons no one understands, the malignant side of human nature occasionally intensifies after death. Thus the ghost of someone who was kind and friendly in life may return as an utterly evil, hateful spirit. Navajo ghosts usually appear as indefinite dark shapes, but they can also travel as whirlwinds or spots of flame. Ghosts pounce on people when they least expect it, tear at their clothes, or throw dirt on them. They haunt the dreams of the living, filling them with dreadful images of sickness and death.

These terrifying visitations, frightful as they are when they happen, are only warnings of worse things to come. Ghosts usually seek out a living person because they want that person to join them. Any

Navajo who sees a ghost, awake or in dreams, knows he or she or a close relative may soon die of ghost-sickness unless curing ceremonies are performed.

Orthodox Navajos know that all illnesses and accidental injuries are supernatural in origin. To bring recovery, the supernatural spirits must be appeased. Atonement must be made for any violations of taboos that the victim may have inadvertently committed. Since there are many, many taboos that must be observed, it is all too easy to make serious mistakes in everyday life. And one should always assume that a malicious ghost —especially one assisted by a witch— will take advantage of the slightest transgression to punish the wayward. If a Navajo passes a shrine or a sacred place without uttering a prayer or making an offering, if corn pollen is not sprinkled when and where it should be, or if "good luck songs" go unsung, the ghosts gain more power.

Fortunately, there are many ways of combatting ghosts and their human accomplices who practice witchcraft. Gall medicine, made from the liver fluids of various animals, is an effective emetic for purging the body of "ghost poisons," while herbs and pollen are both protective and remedial. Ritual sweat baths can purify both the body and the spirit, but the best way to cure ghost-sickness is through ceremonial chanting. Powerful rituals, such as the Evil Way Chant or the Enemy Way Chant, will almost always restore a sick person's health and drive away the menacing spirits.

It is true, of course, that not every phantom is dangerous. Some may simply be disoriented by the new world they have entered; they cannot accept the life of the dead and long to return to the places where they once felt secure and comfortable. Often, it is quite difficult to distinguish between harmless and diabolical

ghosts. A classic example of this dilemma was cited by
Leland C. Wyman in his 1942 research paper, *Navajo
Eschatology*. One of the many Navajos Wyman inter-
viewed told a bizarre tale about a personal encounter
with a ghost which took place while he was a child
attending boarding school. He said that two of his fellow students were practicing the shot put one afternoon on the school's athletic field. Just as one of these
youths threw the heavy steel ball, a group of younger
students raced through. One was struck behind the
ear. Though the youngster was quickly rushed to a
hospital, he never regained consciousness, and died
within a few hours.

On the night after the funeral, his best friend lay
in bed thinking of him. The two boys had bunked side
by side on the porch and had spent many an evening
talking and laughing together. Now, the other bunk
was empty.

About midnight, the saddened youth heard the
screen door creak open. He watched as a dark shape
crossed the porch and sat down on the vacant bed.
With a trembling hand, the boy fumbled for the flashlight under his pillow and directed its beam on the
seated figure. There was no one there. The boy was
thoroughly frightened now. He had never seen a ghost
before, but he remembered all too well the night his
father had ridden home after being attacked by ghosts.
He had come galloping up to the family hogan where
he fell from his horse and lay on the ground in a state
of shock. The medicine man summoned had to sing
most of the night before his father recovered enough to
speak of his harrowing experience.

He told his family that while he was riding
through the darkness, two black creatures rose from
their shadows and came after him. They were on each

side, trying to grab the reins as he rode frantically round and round dodging them. He finally got away, but it was a close call. With that fearful memory in mind, the boy hurried into the dormitory to sleep on the floor amid his fellow students. In the morning, he told them what he had seen on the porch. The other boys helped him carry his bed inside. When night fell again, most of the students sat by the windows, peeking out cautiously. Just as they were beginning to doze, the dark figure reappeared and moved toward the screen door. A dozen flashlights were turned on at once, but, again, whatever had been there vanished instantly.

Now all of the boys agreed it was time to talk to the school superintendent, though they doubted he would believe them. The superintendent was a no-nonsense sort of fellow, and he merely smiled indulgently at the boys' story. "There's no such thing as a ghost," he told them. To prove it, he offered to sleep on the porch himself. "So he did," the deceased boy's friend recalled years later. "And that night he saw somebody coming and he sure ran."

At the earliest opportunity, the boy spoke to his father about the ghostly visitor. "How was your friend buried?" the father asked.

"They dressed him in his school clothes, had a funeral and we all marched, and the band played slow music," the boy answered.

The father nodded knowingly. "That is the reason he returns. He was not buried in the Navajo way, so he cannot go to the Navajo Afterworld. I will speak to a medicine man about this."

A few days later, a rite of passage ceremony was held for the dead boy. A sheep was killed in his honor and his most prized possessions were placed in his grave. After that, the apparition was seen no more.

The incident demonstrated what should have been obvious even back in 1942: only Indian people are capable of dealing with their own spirit world. Sometimes only ancient wisdom prevails, but all too often that wisdom has been neither respected nor understood by non-Indians. This lack of understanding can have serious consequences, as the following tale illustrates.

In 1871, while the Tonto Apache tribe was living on a reservation near Fort Apache, a renegade band of Navajos slipped over the reservation line and stole a herd of Apache ponies. The Apaches pursued the thieves and a pitched battle ensued. Several Navajos were killed but the ponies were recovered. The following day, a powerful Apache medicine man went to the fort to ask Major Phillip Whelan for permission to go to the battlefield and take a scalp from one of the dead Navajos.

The major was appalled. "That is utterly outrageous!" he thundered. "Your people behaved like brave men during the fight, and you should not tarnish their gallant deeds with an act of such barbarism. Stripping a dead enemy of his scalp is an act of atrocious cowardice. I therefore forbid you to go to the battleground for the purpose you have named."

The aged medicine man listened patiently to Major Whalen's diatribe. Then he said, "There is a ceremony that must take place, or the people will be visited by the vengeance of the Great Spirit, Ussen. When one man slays another in battle, the spirit of that dead enemy will haunt the place of his death forever unless the killing is purified. Only one scalp is required to fulfill our obligation."

The major was unconvinced. "Balderdash!" He

turned to the young officer standing stiffly at his side. "Lieutenant, ready your company immediately to frustrate any attempt by any Apache who persists in carrying out this reprehensible charlatan's grisly scheme."

The old medicine man left the command post with the soldiers marching behind him. He walked to the bank of the White River where Apache warriors waited. "The *Nantan* Whelan would not grant my request," he told them. "I am forbidden to use the hair of our enemies in the cleansing rites. Without that, I cannot perform this ceremony properly. But I will do the best I can. Pick up the weapons you used when you fought and follow me."

The medicine man waded into the river's cold, swift current until the water reached his waist. The warriors also entered carrying the arrows they had pulled from the bodies of the dead Navajos. After singing a long incantation, the old man took each warrior's weapons and washed them to remove all bloodstains. Next, he pointed them toward the sky and blew upon the points to waft away the spirits of the dead. When everyone had returned to the shore, the medicine man said, "As you all know, there is more that should have been done. We needed a scalp from which each of you would have taken a few hairs and burned them so the smoke would purify the battleground. Now, we can only hope Ussen will not be angered because we failed to do what has always been required of us."

Soon, winter came to the Tonto reservation and it was one of the worst in years. Many Apaches grew sick and died —a clear sign that Ussen was, indeed, deeply offended. And to compound their troubles, there was much hunger since no one dared go hunting in the direction of the haunted battleground.

Ghosts of this sort pose an eternal threat, but at least they can be avoided as long as people remember where those ghosts are and why they are there. But, sometimes, spirits seem to come out of nowhere and commit terrible deeds for inexplicable reasons. These are the most fearsome spirits, and Arizona's Pima Indians have seen more than their fair share of them.

One of the Pimas' strangest and most oft-repeated tales concerns a terrible creature of this sort. The story, as it is most frequently told, began when an old Pima woman walked down to a pond to fill a water jar. There, to her surprise, she found a beautiful, teenaged girl seated on a rock. The girl was crying, deeply troubled.

"What is wrong?" the old woman asked.

"I am very frightened," the girl replied. "And I have no one to turn to. Both of my parents are dead. I live alone. One night not long ago, a spirit came into my bed. In the morning, I thought it was only a dream, but it was not. I know now that I am pregnant, and I am terrified to think of what may be growing in my womb."

"You had best come with me," the woman decided. "I will look after you. I, too, live alone. Both of my sons are grown and have gone away."

So the girl went to stay in the old woman's home. There, a few months later, her baby was born. Both women were relieved to see that the child was human, but they were shocked that the infant had animal's paws instead of hands and feet. The young mother named her daughter Ho-ok, and cared for her tenderly. But as Ho-ok grew, so did her claws. When she was around other children, Ho-ok would slash at them and make them cry. One day she raked a child's face, disfiguring her permanently. After that, all of the villagers shunned Ho-ok, her mother and the old woman. No one would come near their house, so they lived in near-total isolation.

Ho-ok seemed possessed of a dual personality. Sometimes she was sweet and lovable, delighted to nestle in her mother's arms. On other occasions, she would run shrieking from the house to chase a passing child. One day she caught one, seizing him the way a hawk snares a quail. The screaming boy was badly lacerated before he could be rescued. That night the villagers gathered around a great fire to talk with their shaman.

Ho-ok's mother and the elderly woman crept up as close as they dared, crouching in the shadows. "Can you hear what they are saying?" the mother asked.

"No," the old woman admitted. "I cannot hear their voices, but I know who they are talking about. It is Ho-ok, and I am sure the shaman will decide she must be destroyed. There is only one thing to do now. You must take her to her father."

"But I do not know where he is," she protested.

"Take your child to the pond where I first met you," said the old one. "I feel sure he will be there."

So the young woman went back to the house, awakened her sleeping daughter, took her by the furry paw and led her off into the night. The sun was about to rise when they reached the pond. Although the morning air was still chilly, a heat wave shimmered above the water. "There he is," the young mother said. "That is your father. Leave me now and go to him."

As Ho-ok walked cautiously toward the quivering aura, it rose from the surface of the pond and drifted west into the desert. The little girl followed it as fast as she could, but it always remained just out of reach. For two days, she loped along behind it. When she rested at night, the heat wave waited for her on the horizon, blurring the stars beyond.

On the morning of the third day, the wavering transparency ascended the slope of a boulder-strewn mountain and poised in front of the entrance to a cave. Ho-ok scrambled up the rocks, stepped through a diaphanous veil and entered the dark chamber behind it. She knew at once this was the home of her father, for she could feel his power everywhere. She pressed her paws against the cavern walls, felt the power surge through her; at last she understood who she was destined to become.

For a long time, Ho-ok lived in the cave, absorbing the power and growing. When she reached adolescence, she began prowling the land by night, searching for children who happened to be out after dark. When she caught them, she killed them instantly. All too soon Ho-ok became fully grown, capable of attacking and murdering adults. The death toll rose, and the Pimas lived in perpetual fear.

They looked everywhere for Ho-ok's lair, but found nothing until one morning, just at dawn, a small group of Pimas returning from an all-night search, sighted her entering her secret cave. The Pimas' swiftest runner was sent to the nearest village to rally as many people as possible to come out and help destroy the terrible demon. Scores of Pimas quickly gathered at the base of the peak. Slowly, fearfully, they crept up the slope. The shaman was the first to peek inside.

Ho-ok lay sleeping, curled up on the stony floor. Her paws twitched like those of a dreaming dog. The shaman backed away, then beckoned to the people standing behind him. Without a sound, the Pimas brought great bundles of firewood, bales of straw and baskets of dry grass, piling it in the mouth of the cave. When the entrance was completely sealed, the shaman lit a torch and tossed it in.

Within seconds, the cave was a roaring inferno. The ear-splitting scream that came from inside was so horrifying it sent people scrambling back down the hillside. Flames flashed out of the cracks and crevices above the cave. The peak seemed to shudder as its summit swelled, cracked and burst open, sending a great plume of smoke skyward. Within this billowing cloud, a dark shape twisted and twirled, swooped round and round, flew off toward the horizon and vanished.

The old shaman was trembling uncontrollably. His face was pale with fear. "We have only made things worse," he told the others. "By killing Ho-ok, we released her evil spirit and increased her demonic power. She is more dangerous now than ever before."

Indeed she was. Free now from her body, Ho-ok could transform herself into anything she chose. She could travel as a shadow or fly as a hawk, become nearly invisible, drift like smoke or appear in a fireplace as a glowing ember. No one was safe now, by day or night.

When Ho-ok's killings resumed, the villagers went en masse to the shaman. "Is there nothing we can do to rid ourselves of this merciless fiend?" they asked desperately.

"Even I am not sure," the frightened old man said. "She is terribly clever, but there may be a way to trap her. But it will be very risky. Someone will have to take a water jar and sit with it out in the open where Ho-ok will be sure to see that person. Then, when Ho-ok attacks, that person will have to quickly raise the water jar, catch her in it, and slap the lid on. Who among you will offer to do this?"

The Pimas glanced nervously at one another, each hoping someone else would volunteer. No one did. At last, a woman standing alone at the back of the crowd spoke up. " I will do it," she said.

When the people stepped aside to let her walk through, they saw that it was Ho-ok's mother. Over the years, she had aged more than she should have. Her hair was prematurely grey; a look of perpetual sorrow drenched her eyes. She showed no sign of fear as she accepted the clay pot from the shaman. With all eyes upon her, she strode out into the center of a clearing and settled down to wait.

Less than an hour passed when a dark shadow appeared high in the sky and began circling above the old woman. It swooped lower and lower, suddenly turned into a hawk and with a scream plunged toward her with its talons extended. The old woman waited until the last split-second before she lifted the water jar, captured the hawk and slapped a lid over it.

Villagers who had been hiding nearby ventured out and stood silently as the old woman rose from the ground and handed the jar to the shaman. Then she walked back to her house without speaking.

As the shaman directed, the villagers piled a large stack of firewood on top of the water jar. After the shaman chanted and shook his gourd rattle, they ignited a fire that blazed for three days. When the ashes cooled, the shaman instructed that the jar be buried deep in the ground. Two men picked up the blackened urn but when they heard something scratching around inside, they dropped it and ran. The jar split open, the lid rolled away and dozens of poisonous insects —scorpions, black widows, centipedes and tarantulas— came swarming out, scurrying off in all directions.

Still Ho-ok had not been completely destroyed. True, the chanting and burning had taken away most of her power. She could no longer fly through the sky nor tear people apart with her claws, but her spirit was now scattered far and wide within the earth's lowliest creatures. She remains forever ready to sting or bite anyone careless enough to brush away a spider web with a bare hand or to put on a shoe without first shaking it out.

Ho-ok is not the only unconquerable evil spirit menacing Arizona's Indian country. Many other fearsome creatures lurk in the more remote parts of the reservations. Over the years, people have learned it is best to just leave them alone, to stay away from them and never, *ever* antagonize them. A young Navajo boy, John C. Claw, learned that lesson in the summer of 1941. He was nine years old at the time, old enough to be a sheep herder. His cousin, a year older, was already an experienced shepherd, so before the two boys drove their flock to a mountain meadow, the cousin gave John some important advice.

"There are some very bad things that live in these mountains," he explained. "But you'll never see one of them unless you call out its name. Its name is 'Shash'. So remember, cousin, never say that word while we are in the mountains. If you do, a *Shash* will come after you for sure."

Nervously, John promised to remember. At daybreak the two boys herded their sheep up to the pasture. Throughout the morning, John Claw thought about what his cousin had said. By noon, he was feeling a bit peeved. "He's playing a joke on me," John concluded. "Just trying to scare me. He thinks that because he's older, he's smarter than I am. Well, I'll show him I can play jokes, too."

John Claw's cousin was sitting on the uphill side of the meadow near the tree line, watching the flock. Young John tip-toed up behind him, bent down and shouted in his ear: "A *Shash!* A *Shash!* Look out, here comes a *Shash!*"

The cousin jumped to his feet, wide-eyed with fear. "Why did you say that?" he demanded. "Do you want to get us killed?"

John giggled merrily. "You thought you fooled me, but I know there's no such thing as a *Shash*," he said. But suddenly a deep, grunting roar rumbled down from the forest above. Both boys froze in their tracks, while the sheep dogs dashed off into the timber, barking wildly. Moments later, one of the dogs yelped in pain and the other's bark was a lot less brave than before.

"We've got to go get our dogs," the cousin cried, "or the *Shash* will kill them. Come on, John. Don't just stand there!"

Reluctantly, the shaken little boy followed the older one through the thick brush until they came to a small opening in the forest. There a great black beast stood on its hind legs, bellowing at the dogs. "Oh, no!" groaned the cousin, "This time the *Shash* has turned itself into a bear."

John Claw had never seen a bear before, but he knew this was no ordinary bear. It was enormous. It picked up rocks to throw at the dogs and swung a big stick. John's cousin yelled at the frenzied dogs, ordering them to return. When they finally did, the terrified boys ran pell-mell back down the slope with the bruised and battered canines limping behind them. They wasted no time in rounding up the flock and herding them back down the mountain.

John C. Claw swore his story was true, and

assured that he never again, in all his future years as a shepherd, ever uttered the word *"Shash"* while he was in the mountains.

With or without the added peril of *Shash*, bears are considered awesome creatures by many Native Americans. While all animals possess certain supernatural powers, bears are usually given much respect and a wide berth. Any contact with a bear can cause "bear sickness," an ailment with serious effects. It has been described as feeling like something is creeping through your body and poking its way into the heart. Hunters who kill bears are in very serious risk of contracting bear sickness. In fact, even the breath of a bear should be avoided, since it goes directly to one's lungs.

Owls must also be taken seriously. To the Navajos, the owl is the perfect symbol of death, since it can both predict and cause the end of a person's life. It is extremely unwise to look directly into the eyes of an owl or to touch an owl feather, since either can bring very bad luck or result in a terminal illness. Whenever an owl hoots near a hogan, it is a sure sign that someone in the family will soon die.

For the Apaches, warnings of impending death usually come from coyotes. Irene Burlison, a former teacher for the Bureau of Indian Affairs, once related a story told to her by an Apache woman during the early 1950s. The woman said a coyote came near her house and howled several nights in a row. The following night, there was no coyote howl, but it was the night her sister died. Within hours of the sister's death, her father came hurrying home from the mountain cabin where he herded cattle. He said he had gone to bed for the night when he was awakened by a coyote coming into the room. The coyote put its front paws on the foot of the bed and told him his daughter was dying.

This special relationship between humans and animals is highly regarded by all traditional Indian people who have a deep respect for the spiritual nature of animals, birds, reptiles and fish.

In 1977, when the Navajo Tribal government decided to establish a tribal zoo in the Navajo capital, Window Rock, many Navajo elders were disturbed. It offended the dieties to see animals imprisoned and their spirits confined, they said. Also, since some animals have evil spirits, they could pose a threat to zoo visitors. Several important medicine men convened for long talks with the Navajo Tribal Parks and Recreation officials. During these discussions, they learned that nearly all of the zoo's display animals would be those which could never be returned to the wild. They were mostly birds of prey with crippled wings, mule deer that had lived in captivity since they were fawns, and a cougar with a hip problem. In a zoo these animals could be kept alive and healthy.

Given these assurances, the medicine men agreed to approve of the menagerie provided they were allowed to perform a prayer ceremony to bless all of the animals. So it was that the Navajo Nation Zoological and Botanical Park was dedicated on July 4, 1977, thus becoming the first tribal zoo in the country to be licensed by the U.S. Department of Agriculture.

Navajos come to the zoo from all parts of their vast reservation, often bringing corn pollen to sprinkle on the animals. If, for example, a person sprinkles pollen on a roadrunner, that person will be able to run faster.

The zoo's curator, Loline Hathaway, tells of an old man with a severe breathing problem who visited the zoo on several occasions to shake pollen on a bull-snake. Hathaway believes the ritual actually helped the old gentleman. "His health did improve," she insists. One of the zoo keepers remembers a time during the fall of 1990 when an aged medicine man asked him to get a cougar whisker needed for a healing ceremony. "How on earth am I going to pull a whisker off that 200-pound cat?" the keeper asked.

As luck would have it, old Candy the Cougar was scheduled for surgery on an impacted tooth within a few days. Once the mountain lion was tranquilized, the zoo keeper plucked a single whisker off its muzzle. The whisker was presented to the medicine man who was assured of a successful ceremony.

Surely the most sacred creature of all is the mighty eagle. Its strength, keen vision and ability to soar high above the earth proves it possesses spiritual powers of mythic proportions. The feathers of these great birds are highly prized; whether they are from the long, sky-slashing tips of the wings or the soft, downy fluff on the body, the eagle feathers play an important, indeed essential, part in many ceremonies.

However, it is a violation of federal law to possess eagle feathers without a permit, so legally it is not permitted to pick up feathers at the Navajo Tribal Zoo. Instead Hathaway gathers up the feathers shed by eagles and gives them to Navajo Fish and Wildlife officials who can then distribute them to qualified seekers. These feathers are especially valuable since, having come from living birds, they hold even more spiritual power than those from dead birds.

The spirit world of Arizona's Indian people is wondrous and incredibly complex. Though it is largely unseen and often filled with terrible dangers, it shapes the lives of all who live and believe in the traditional ways. The spirit world is always there, always has been, always will be. Perhaps a single line from an ancient Navajo protection-song sums it up: "Among the alien gods with weapons of magic am I."

How To Visit the Sacred Animals

The Navajo Nation Zoological and Botanical Park is part of the Tse Bonito Tribal Park on the eastern edge of Window Rock, north of Highway 264, and less than a quarter of a mile west of the New Mexico-Arizona state line. The park is open every day except Christmas and New Year's Day from 8 a.m. to 5 p.m. A shade house and picnic tables are available if you wish to bring a lunch and enjoy a very special setting. Accompanying the animal collection are the botanical exhibits representing two dozen species of native plants, and an indoor section that allows you to see many of the desert's smaller creatures.

As you stroll about, resist the temptation to pick up eagle feathers, avoid the stare of the horned owls and don't let the bear breathe on you.

Bibliography - Chapter 5

Bahr, Donald M. Gregorio, Juan; Lopez, David and Alvarez, Albert. **Piman Shamanism and Staying Sickness.** Tucson. The University of Arizona Press. 1974.

Cremony, John C. **Life Among the Apaches.** San Francisco. A. Roman & Company. 1868.

Haile, Berard. **Legend of the Ghostway Ritual.** St. Michaels, Arizona. Saint Michaels Press. 1950.

Hillinger, Charles. *Los Angeles Times.* August 26, 1990.

Kluckhorn, Clyde and Leighton, Dorothea. **The**

Navajo. Cambridge, Massachusetts. Harvard University Press. 1974.

Saxton, Dean and Lucille. **Legends and Lore of the Papago and Pima Indians.** Tucson. The University of Arizona Press. 1973.

Young, Robert W. and Morgan, William. **Navajo Historical Selections.** Phoenix. Phoenix Indian School Indian Print Shop. 1954.

6

Massacre at Wickenburg

On November 5, 1871, the eastbound mail wagon from Krug's Wells to Wickenburg was rolling along right on time. Its spinning wheels churned the dust while the driver rocking back and forth on the wooden seat stared dully at the desolate Arizona landscape. At his side, a shotgun-guard dozed restlessly; his head snapped up and fell back with each new jolt in the road.

The Wickenburg mail run was long and lonely back in 1871 —thirty miles of wheel ruts across the empty desert between Vulture Peaks and the Date Creek Mountains. There was little to relieve the monotony, so a man could easily become mesmerized by the endless wasteland. Then, thirteen miles out of Wickenburg, the driver sat bolt upright in his seat and drew in hard on the reins.

On the shimmering horizon, two human figures

had suddenly appeared, lurching unsteadily forward. Instantly the guard, too, came awake, squinting down the road, cocking his shotgun. In Arizona Territory in 1871, the sudden appearance of human beings in the middle of nowhere always meant trouble —one way or another.

When the approaching figures caught sight of the buckboard, they began running toward it, frantically waving until one of them abruptly pitched over in the dust. "They're hurt!" the driver exclaimed, as he watched the tall figure struggle to get up. "And, my god, that one's a woman!"

He slapped the reins and the horses lunged ahead, quickly closing the gap between themselves and the staggering couple. The mail wagon slid to a halt. A dust cloud drifted over the two most pathetic figures either man had ever seen. Both were badly wounded. Their clothes were soaked with blood and sweat. They had been running for miles and were now barely able to speak as they blurted out their tale of horror. They were the sole survivors of what was soon to become known nationwide as the Wickenburg Massacre.

The male survivor was William Kruger. The woman was Miss Mollie Shepard of Prescott. Even with the blood and grime on her face, the mail-runners could still clearly discern her beauty. Miss Mollie was well-known in that part of Arizona; she was one of the Territory's most popular practitioners of the world's oldest profession.

The mail-runners did what they could to make the injured pair comfortable. They hurriedly built a make-shift barricade, carried the victims inside and, while the guard knelt beside them with his shotgun at the ready, the driver cut loose a horse and rode for help. It was midnight before he returned bringing a doctor and an armed posse from town. Mollie Shepard and William Kruger were soon on their way to safety, scarcely able to believe they were still alive.

News of the massacre spread quickly through the small desert town. The Wickenburg stagecoach had been ambushed, and the driver, the guard and all the passengers except Kruger and Shepard had been killed. Kruger said the stage had been attacked at 8 a.m. by ten, possibly eleven assailants. The ambushers had first shot the lead horse, then methodically riddled the stalled coach with rifle fire. Although he and Miss Mollie had both been hit, they managed to get out and run away.The ambushers had spotted them as they fled and pursued them briefly before turning back to begin looting the stagecoach. Why hadn't the outlaws finished them off? Kruger didn't know. Perhaps they were out of ammunition, he suggested. Were they Indians? Kruger was positive they were, but Mollie Shepard was not so sure about that.

Captain Charles Meinhold was summoned from Camp Date Creek to lead a detachment of the Third Cavalry to the site of the atrocity. There they found the coach standing as the attackers had left it —one horse was dead on the ground, the others drooped in their harnesses. Scattered in and around the stagecoach lay seven bodies, and 17 bullet holes were counted in the side of the coach. Moccasin tracks were everywhere, all reportedly "of the pattern used by Apache Mojaves."

Curiously, none of the luggage had been disturbed. No trunk, valise or hat box had been opened. Nor had any bodies been searched. In every case, pocket watches, rings and wallets were left behind. Only the mail pouch had been opened. The contents of the pouch were strewn on the ground, but oddly, only one envelope had been opened —not ripped apart, but carefully slit at one end. It was an official letter addressed to "A.Q.M."

Captain Meinhold slapped the envelope against the palm of his gloved hand. "Army Quartermaster," he said. "Damnation! This coach was carrying the Army payroll!" Meinhold ordered his men to search the stage for the strongbox but, as he fully expected, it was long gone.

"Just how much money would there have been in that box, sir?" a trooper asked.

"More than you'll ever see in your lifetime, soldier," the captain replied. "Close to $100,000."

Meinhold's troops set off on the outlaws' trail, following the tracks nearly all the way to the banks of Hassavampa Creek, southeast of the Vultures. Here they lost the trail.

Back in Wickenburg, Mollie Shepard was sufficiently recovered from her ordeal to begin enjoying the publicity she had earned. A continuous stream of male admirers called at the plucky young woman's bedside to marvel at her courage and wish her a speedy recovery. Then, inevitably, they all asked the same question: "Was it an Indian massacre, Mollie?"

Miss Mollie shook her golden curls. "No," she said. "I don't think so." She related a strange incident that occurred just before she boarded the stage in Prescott. A man she had never seen before approached her. Polite and courteous, he asked where she was going. "Wickenburg," she had replied. "And is the stage carrying a lot of money?" he asked.

"I really couldn't say," Mollie had answered. The man tipped his hat, smiled knowingly and disappeared into the crowd. A meaningless encounter perhaps, but who could say for sure?

Captain Meinhold returned to the scene of the

crime and made a thorough search of the area. He found, among other things, two butter tins, a pack of Spanish playing cards, and a small shovel hidden behind some rocks. In those days, tin cans were often used by Indians as water canteens, and three-card monte games were enjoyed by Apaches and Mexicans alike. And, it goes without saying, shovels have sometimes been used to bury strongboxes. This meager evidence proved nothing; it could have been left by Indians, Mexican bandits, or it could have been deliberately planted.

Meinhold was more interested in the fact that the stagecoach horses had been left behind. No Apache marauder had ever been known to pass up an opportunity to steal horses. Inside the coach, blankets and lap robes lay untouched, along with the fancy window curtains. Would Apaches overlook such delectable treasures? Meinhold thought it highly unlikely. But if it was not an Indian attack, why had there been so many murders?

Stagecoach robberies were certainly not uncommon on the Arizona frontier, but they were usually committed without the loss of lives. Why did the perpetrators of this particular holdup feel it necessary to attempt to kill everyone on board? Meinhold and the other investigators wondered if the fact that five of the victims were prominent citizens was a factor in that cold-blooded decision.

Three of the dead were members of the famous Wheeler survey party. The fourth was a wealthy businessman named Adams, and the fifth was Frederick W. Loring, a well-known eastern writer. A good many Arizonans were not unhappy to hear of Loring's death. He was one of those "damned outsiders" whose articles were considered entirely sympathetic to the Indian tribes of the Territory. If he had, in fact, been murdered by the "noble savages" whose cause he championed, then a lot of folks agreed it was an appropriate fate for him.

The massacre could not have come at a worse time. Vincent Colyer, secretary of the Federal Board of Peace Commissioners, was currently touring Arizona, holding councils with Indian leaders, attempting to "locate the nomadic tribes on suitable reservations" and, through peaceful settlements, bring the bitter Indian wars to a close. A large part of the white populace of Arizona vehemently opposed Colyer's mission. They were thoroughly convinced that only the total extermination of the hostile tribes could secure the frontier. The Wickenburg Massacre now served as a graphic example of the Arizonans' dilemma. If such important figures could be killed at random, then no one was safe from the Indian menace.

"Colyer's peace efforts have failed," the *Prescott Miner* editorialized. "We are still at the mercy of bloodthirsty savages!"

Captain Meinhold turned in his report to General George R. Crook, commander of the Arizona Department of the Army at Fort Whipple. He expressed his belief that the massacre was "a scheme planned for some time," and acknowledged that "many people accuse the Indians living at the Date Creek Agency." Meinhold added that he thought the solution to the crime was not that simple.

General Crook pondered the problem. Although he often disagreed with Secretary Colyer, he, too, believed a peaceful settlement to the Indian problem was possible. Still, he knew the Wickenburg Massacre further jeopardized an already volatile situation. The guilty parties —whoever they were— would have to be brought to justice. But how? Every clue seemed to lead to a dead end; the investigation was going nowhere. Then, late in January 1872, a small group of Date Creek Apaches entered the Colorado River Mojave Reservation and contacted a young Indian named Iretaba.

The Apaches had been drinking; they were cocky and boastful. They produced an enormous sum of paper money and asked Iretaba how much it was. The young Mojave had been raised by a white scout, Dan O'Leary, and was fairly well-educated. He counted the money and handed it back.

"It is almost 100,000 dollars," Iretaba told them. The reveling Indians went whooping off into the night. Next day, Iretaba and several sub-chiefs went to Fort Whipple to talk to General Crook. Their story convinced the general that Apaches had, indeed, taken part in the massacre. If these Indians could be apprehended and interrogated, Crook felt sure they would reveal the masterminds behind the crime. Could Iretaba identify the suspect Indians if he confronted them again?

Iretaba was certain he could. In fact, he said, one of the Apaches was already well known to him. He was Ochacama, chief of the Date Creeks.

The Date Creek Agency was one of the most dismal, sickly and poorly managed reservations in all Arizona. The Indians herded there were on the verge of desperation. They had tried the white man's "peaceful cultivation" and nearly starved. Consequently, their young men still rode forth on raids. Now, apparently, they had somehow managed to pull off a raid of historic proportions.

General Crook began devising an elaborate plan to capture the suspects. He proposed a peace confer-

ence between himself and the irreconcilable elements
of the tribe. He requested that Iretaba accompany him
to his conference to hand out gifts —short twists of
black tobacco— at the start of the talks. But Iretaba
was to give the gifts only to the Indians who had shown
him the money. Once the suspects had been so identified, soldiers escorting General Crook would casually
move in alongside these marked men and stand ready
to seize them at a given signal. Had it not been for the
incredibly complex relationship existing between white
man and red, the plot might have succeeded as
planned.

The Date Creek Apaches were not long in learning of Crook's scheme. Perhaps word came to them
from informers within General Cook's Indian scouts.
Just as the general maintained a network of informers
throughout the hostile bands, so the renegade Apaches
had informants of their own among his Indian auxil-
iaries. With spies operating on both sides, no secret
remained covert for long.

Ochacama quickly formulated a counter-plan.
"Let the general come to us," he told his braves. "And
let us welcome him and pretend to listen to his words.
When he has been lulled, when his guard is down,
then we will strike. The *Nantan* Crook plans to seal our
fate with twists of tobacco, so let it be tobacco that sig-
nals his death instead. All of you will watch me. When
the time is right, you will see me light a cigarette. At
the first puff of smoke, raise your rifles and fire. We
will kill the *Nantan* and all who come here with him.

"Once he is dead, we will leave this cursed place.
We will take our people and flee into the hills, to the
canyons beyond the Santa Maria, where no white man
can follow."

Perhaps Ochacama did not realize the enormity

GENERAL GEORGE R. CROOK. Apaches suffered retaliation, but who really committed the Wickenburg Massacre of 1871?

of the deed he proposed. The assassination of an American general would have rocked the nation from coast to coast, bringing reprisals which might well have wiped out the already endangered Apache nation. But before the trap could be sprung, the secret leaked out. This time, it was the friendly Hualapais who passed word of Ochacama's intrigue to General Crook. The general hesitated only briefly before electing to proceed with his original plan. He altered his strategy only in one respect: instead of soldiers, his escort would be made up of mule packers.

Crook's mule packers were a special breed. As Captain John Gregory Brourke pointed out in his reminesences: "These were 'men' in the truest sense of the term; they had faced all perils, endured all privations, and conquered in a manly way." In short, they were the saltiest dogs on the frontier. With them as body guards, General Crook feared no evil.

Shortly before the explosive "peace" conference was to take place, Captain Phillip Dwyer, Fifth Cavalry, commander of the Date Creek Post, was stricken ill and died rather abruptly. John G. Bourke assumed his command, and General Crook rode out to Date Creek sooner than the Indians expected. Crook sent word to Ochacama: "We will talk on the morrow."

Ochacama was more than ready.

Next day, at mid-morning, the Apaches assembled at the pre-designated site. They had ceremoniously painted their faces, and all were fully armed. Soon Crook arrived and Ochacama was pleased to note he was escorted by a mere handful of soldiers. The Apache chief paid scant attention to the rough-looking civilians who seemed to be there only for the purpose of tending the horses.

The Indians seated themselves in a semi-circle

facing the whites and casually laid their rifles across their laps. Crook nodded at Iretaba, who began handing out the fateful twists of tobacco. Ochacama frowned as he noticed a packer slipping in behind each man who received a gift.

When Iretaba extended a twist to Ochacama, the chieftain shook his head. Iretaba insisted, so Ochacama accepted the gift, then cast it to the ground. "I have tobacco of my own," he said, producing a pouch and paper. There was dead silence as the Apache leader slowly began rolling a cigarette.

He glanced at his warriors, struck a match and exhaled a cloud of smoke. Instantly, an Apache rifle flashed up and fired at General Crook. In the same instant, a packer's shoulder crashed against the warrior's arm as a second packer knocked Crook to the ground. The bullet went wild and the general was safe for the moment. Another soldier made dive at the nearest Indian and received a fatal knife thrust to the stomach. Everyone was on his feet now, swinging, slashing, grabbing at the rifles. Hank Hewitt, a muleteer of monstrous size, seized the biggest Indian he could find. They crashed to the earth locked in mortal combat. Kicking, clawing, biting, they fought until Hewitt managed to grasp the Apache's ears and smash his skull on a rock.

General Crook himself leaped into the fray, kicking rifles aside and shouting for order. The brawl was hopelessly out of control. As Captain Bourke would later write, it was "a perfect Kilkenny fight." Pistols roared, fists thumped and "many of the party were killed or wounded."

Three men tackled Ochacama and were barely able to hold him down while his wrists were tied. Seven Apaches died in the donney-brook while the rest fled

the reservation. Ochacama was dragged screaming to
the crude shack that served as a guard house. His
brother was already imprisoned there on a gun-smug-
gling charge. When he heard Ochacama bellowing his
rage in the next cell, he went berserk. He grabbed a
roof beam and swung his feet at the canvas ceiling. He
burst through, hit the ground and was attempting to
kick open Ochacama's door when a volley of bullets cut
him down.

Inside, Ochacama had broken his bonds and was
furiously hurtling old boots, wash basins and curses at
the guards. When his brother fell dead, Ochacama
flung himself through the canvas wall and attacked the
guards barehanded. A trooper's bayonet pierced his
side, but the Indian chief pulled himself free and made
a wild dash for the hills. Bullets sang about his heels
as he disappeared from sight.

Ochacama's escape now led to a general exodus
of the hard-core renegades from Date Creek. These
angry warriors took their families and assembled in the
rugged ravines of the Muchos Cañones area, northwest
of the reservation. Here, where the five forks of the
Santa Maria join, Ochacama nursed his wound and
plotted his revenge. He blamed Iretaba for everything
and swore he would be killed in a war of revenge
against the Mojave Apaches.

A few weeks later, the peaceful Hualapais
brought word to General Crook of Ochacama's proposed retaliation. Crook quickly dispatched three companies of the Fifth Cavalry along with 80 Hualapai
Indian scouts to Mucho Cañones. The troopers made a
42-mile forced march in three days, following the
Hualapai over torturously rough Burro Creek Trail to
the Apache encampments. Crawling on their hands
and knees, they surrounded the *rancherias*. Just

before dawn, they launched their attack.

Lieutenant Walter S. Schuyler later described the action in a letter to his father: "We jumped up and poured a withering crossfire on the astonished hostiles. The few warriors who were not knocked over made for the canyon, where Michler's men picked them off from the opposite side. We killed about 40 Indians, captured a large number of children and eight squaws."

The battle of Mucho Cañones ended the long, bloody episode which began with a stagecoach robbery and nearly resulted in the assassination of an American general. All told, the chain of events cost nearly 60 lives. The mystery of the original massacre, however, was never solved. Did the Date Creek Apaches themselves plan and execute the robbery? This seemly highly improbable. But, if white men were involved, why did the Apaches wind up with all the loot? One conclusion seems inescapable.

Ochacama was an incredibly wild man capable of committing any treachery in the forlorn hope of helping his beleaguered people. Is it not conceivable that, following the robbery, he would slay his white accomplices and take the money for himself? If so, what happened to all that money? None of it was ever recovered.

It would seem logical for the Date Creeks to have hidden the money before their meeting with Crook, probably by burying it, just as they must have buried the white outlaws corpses, somewhere in a place that has never been discovered. No one will ever know for sure who committed the Wickenburg Massacre, but it is safe to say that no one profited from this horrendous deed. Everyone involved may well have paid for the crime with their lives.

How to Visit the Site of the Wickenburg Massacre

A few miles west of Wickenburg on Highway 60, at the entrance road to the Flying E Ranch, is a stone monument built by the Arizona Highway Department in 1937. The monument is not on the exact site of the massacre which actually occurred approximately 1.5 miles to the northwest, along the old Wickenburg-Ehrenberg stage route. However, you can see the wild brush landscape across which Mollie Shepard and William Kruger ran for their lives. (The monument's plaque incorrectly states that Mollie Shepard died of her wounds.)

To the north, the Date Creek Mountains are visible on the horizon. Perhaps somewhere out in those wild, desolate hills, the loot from Arizona's most famous stagecoach robbery is still buried.

Bibliography - Chapter 6

Colyer, Vincent. **Peace With The Apaches of New Mexico and Arizona.** Washington DC. Government Printing Office. 1872.

Miller, Joseph. **The Arizona Story.** New York. Hastings House. 1952.

Schellie, Don. **Vast Domain of Blood.** New York. Tower Books. 1971.

Thrapp, Dan L. **The Conquest of Apacheria.** Norman, Oklahoma. University of Oklahoma Press. 1967.

Williams, Brad and Pepper, Choral. **Lost Legends of the West.** New York. Holt, Rinehart & Winston. 1970.

7

Mysteries of the Grand Canyon

On April 18, 1858, Lieutenant Joseph C. Ives stood on the rim of the Grand Canyon and stared at the chasm in disgust. "This region is altogether valueless," he told the weary surveyors, geologists and artists standing beside him. "Ours will doubtless be the last party of whites to visit this profitless locality. It seems intended by nature that the Colorado River along the greater part of its lonely and majestic way, shall be forever unvisited and undisturbed. There is nothing to do but leave, and probably none will follow us."

Never in the history of Arizona has anyone been so completely, utterly, dead wrong. During the years since Lieutenant Ives' unsuccessful attempt to explore the canyon for the federal Office of Explorations and

Surveys, the number of people —white, black, brown,
red and yellow people— who have visited and sometimes disturbed this magnificent site soars well into
the millions. Most of these visitors have been content
to stand on the rim and experience the heady rush of
vertigo and acrophobia that comes with that first
glance into the earth's ultimate chasm. Countless others who have stared into this gorge have been drawn
irresistibly into its depths, down its precipitous slopes
into the heart of its grandeur. Long before there were
maps or trails, people were entering the canyon for a
wide variety of reasons.

More than 3,000 years ago, hunters and gatherers were living in caves in the canyon's walls; the Hopis
made annual trips to the salt beds for at least a thousand years, and, of course, the Havasupai Indians still
live there.

In 1540, 13 members of the Spanish exploration
led by Francisco Vasquez de Coronado became the first
Europeans to gaze over the brink, searching for a way
to cross it south to north. They failed even to reach the
inner gorge, for its cliffs, which from above looked no
taller than the walls of Spanish castles, proved to be
vertical escarpments hundreds of feet high. The *Con-
quistadores* were bold men, but they knew there was
no way they could breach the defenses of this unassail-
able canyon, nor conquer the wild river roaring
through it. Defeated, they returned to Mexico; the
advance of the Spanish empire went in other directions.

Three centuries passed before any other Europeans showed a serious interest in the Grand Canyon.
A few Franciscan missionaries rode their donkeys by it
on their way to the villages of the Hopis and the Zunis,
but it was not until the early 1800s that small parties

of trappers and prospectors began venturing into the chasm itself. However, due to the incredible enormity of the canyon, their observations were very limited and were confined primarily to the more accessible areas.

Overall, the Grand Canyon continued to be a very mysterious realm, an enigma so deep and wide that it was commonly believed no bird smaller than an eagle could fly across it. It was also believed no human being could possibly ride through the canyon in a boat and survive.

If the canyon itself was awe-inspiring, its river —the furious, rampaging Colorado— was utterly intimidating. There were rumors of waterfalls as tumultuous as Niagara, and whirlpools so big they could swallow a boat of any size in an instant. Some folks claimed the river went underground at one point and came bursting back out many miles downstream. Certainly, no one in his right mind would challenge the mighty Colorado.

Undeniably, the Colorado is a mighty river. From its headwaters in the Rocky Mountains to its mouth on the Gulf of California, it travels over 1,200 miles, draining an area of some 244,000 square miles. In the 285-mile stretch through the Grand Canyon, between Lee's Ferry and what is now Lake Mead, there are 81 rapids. Most of those are real stomach-churners even in the improved rafts of today. Lava Falls Rapid, for example, has a 37-foot drop in elevation, and leaves rafters feeling as if they had just gone down a roller-coaster inside a washing machine. Running the river today may be a giant thrill, but a hundred years ago, it was a death-defying odyssey that no one took for the fun of it.

Lieutenant Ives was the first to give it a try, although it was hardly for fun. Bureaucrats back in

Washington authorized and outfitted an expedition to determine whether the Colorado was navigable. None of those bureaucrats had ever been west of the Mississippi, so their knowledge of truly wild rivers was non-existent. They assumed the right vessel to make a voyage up the Colorado would be a paddle-wheel steamboat.

At least they allowed the lieutenant to decide what kind of boat he needed. Ives personally supervised the building of a special, bright red, 54-foot craft which he then tested on the peaceful Delaware River. He christened this fine little boat "Explorer," and ordered it shipped in sections to Panama.

Then the crated boat sections were transported by rail to the Pacific Ocean where *Explorer* was shipped to San Francisco. It was re-loaded again onto the deck of a two-masted schooner which sailed all the way back down the coast to the southern tip of Baja California and then up the Gulf of California where it finally reached the muddy delta of the Colorado River.

By this time, December 1, 1857, *Explorer* had traveled piggyback more than 8,000 miles. Now the time had come for it to head out on its own, to fight its way upstream like a spawning salmon.

With considerable difficulty, Ives and his crew reassembled and launched their fragile boat. The first part of the voyage, north from Fort Yuma to the mouth of the Grand Canyon, was arduous and slow, but not really pioneering; a few other steamers had already struggled upstream that far, so Ives knew his craft could do the same. On January 30, 1858, Ives' spunky vessel passed the previous head of navigation and paddled valiantly into the unknown. Twenty-four hours later, it came to an abrupt, screeching halt.

Ives got no farther than the juncture of Black

COLORADO RIVER. The Grand Canyon's unexplored depths lured many adventurers to strange and often tragic fates.

Canyon and Grand Canyon before *Explorer's* bow was split by an enormous submerged rock.The impact was so powerful that everyone on the forward deck was catapulted into the water, and the men on the afterdeck were thrown into the machinery. The entire wheelhouse was ripped off; the boiler popped its support bolts and the smokestack tilted crazily.

The boat's pilot, a bear of a man named David Robinson, assessed the damage and shook his shaggy head. "We're takin' on water," he reported. "I'm afraid she's done for, Lieutenant."

The fanatical side of Ives' nature surfaced. "Not yet, she isn't!" he shouted. "Not until she's gone further up this cursed river than any other boat has ever gone! Or ever will go!"

He nursed this mortally wounded craft on upstream until he reached what he thought was the Virgin River. There he abandoned *Explorer* on a sandbar. He and his crew climbed out of the canyon, having done their best. Perhaps this was the best of possible outcomes. One shudders to think what would have happened if Ives had reached Lava Falls Rapid.

A decade passed before another expedition was organized to run the Colorado. The man who headed this excursion was uniquely suited to the task. He was tenacious, adventurous, stubborn and brilliant. His name was John Wesley Powell.

As the son of an abolitionist Methodist preacher, young Powell got into so many fistfights defending his family's anti-slavery views that he was kicked out of the public schools and had to be privately tutored. At the age of 18, he became a teacher himself.

A few years later, he fell in love with his cousin, Emma Dean. Despite objections from both families, they married on November 28, 1861. Powell was in the army at the time, serving as a second lieutenant under General Ulysses S. Grant. During the battle of Shiloh, his right arm was shattered by a bullet. It was amputated just below the shoulder two days later. This painful mutilation would have ended the military career of a lesser man, but the daring young lieutenant returned to combat, and rose to the rank of major. He commanded an artillery battalion until the end of the Civil War.

With hostilities ended, the discharged veteran found teaching a bit too tame for his restless nature. The West beckoned irresistibly. In the summer of 1867, with the equally adventurous Emma at his side, he led his first expedition into the Rocky Mountains to collect geologic and botanic specimens for universities in the East. It was there, high in the glorious alpine watershed of the Colorado River, that a dream began to grow in his mind —a dream so grandiose that if he succeeded in making it a reality, it would assure him a place in history alongside all the other great explorers of the American West.

John Wesley Powell decided to be the first person to take an expedition down the entire length of the Colorado, from its northernmost headwaters to the salt waters of the Gulf of California. It would be the wildest river run of all time.

Powell spent the better part of the next year seeking financial backing. With the help of his friend, President Ulysses S. Grant, he raised the necessary funds to get outfitted. On May 24, 1869, he and a crew of nine men launched four large, specially-built boats at Green River, Wyoming. As townspeople cheered, the awkward little flotilla drifted off downstream. The low, sturdy, round-bottomed boats were double-ribbed with cured oak. Each was loaded with two tons of supplies and equipment in waterproof bulkheads. Powell went first in the *Emma Dean*, scouting the way and giving names to the side canyons and mountains as he passed them.

The Powell expedition hit its first rough water at Ladore Canyon in Utah. Suddenly the slyly peaceful Green River became a boiling torrent. Powell, from his vantage position, signaled for the boats behind him to pull into shore. But the boat called *No Name* responded too slowly. Within seconds, it went from a speed of two miles an hour to 20. It spun like a top before exploding into kindling wood when it hit the rocks. All three crew members were swept away; miraculously, they washed onto a tiny island from which they were rescued.

The accident was a sobering experience, to say the least. The expedition was only 16 days out of Green River and already one boat was lost along with 4,000 pounds of supplies, and a third of the men had nearly drowned. Powell named the rapids "Disaster Falls" and pushed on. The flotilla reached the confluence of the Green River and the Colorado on June 16. From there, they raced through 64 rapids in Cataract Canyon, passed Lee's Ferry, and entered the Grand Canyon. "We have but a month's rations remaining," Powell wrote in his journal. "And, we are three-quarters of a mile into the depths of the earth."

Powell's journal, which was later published as *Canyons of the Colorado*, eloquently described the group's plunge through "the great Unknown." A sample passage from the book reveals what the trip was like:

"The river is very deep, the canyons very narrow and obstructed, so that there is no steady flow of the stream, but the waters wheel, and roll, and boil, and we are scarcely able to determine where we can go. Now the boat is carried to the right, perhaps close to the wall; again, she is shot into the stream, and perhaps dragged over to the other side, where, caught in a whirlpool, she spins about. We can neither land nor run as we please. The boats are entirely unmanageable; now one, now another is ahead, each crew laboring for its own preservation.

"In such a place we come to another rapid. Two of the boats run it perforce. One succeeds in landing, but there is no foothold by which to make portage, and she is pushed out again into the stream. The next minute a great reflex wave fills the open compartment; she is waterlogged and drifts unmanageable. Breaker after breaker rolls over her, and one capsizes her. The men are thrown out; but they cling to the boat, and she drifts down some distance, alongside of us, and we are able to catch her. She is soon bailed out and the men are aboard once more."

Half-way through this wild, unpredictable maelstrom, three crewmen decided they had had enough; they bid Powell goodbye and trekked out of the canyon. They died in the empty country to the south. The rest of the party lunged ahead, riding the rapids like cowboys on broncs, then coasting through the placid stretches singing loud songs that bounded back from the towering cliffs. At the end of August, they reached the Mormon town of Callville, where Lake Mead now stands, and stepped triumphantly ashore.

Powell became a national hero as newspapers across the land told of the one-armed man who was the first ever to successfully take a boat through the Grand Canyon. But almost immediately, his claim to fame was challenged. Scores of people swore he was *not* the first, that there had been another before him, a man who, all by himself, had survived a run through the Grand Canyon.

Citizens of Callville remembered a day in September 1867 when a crude raft was sighted coming out of the canyon. The pathetic figure clinging to the raft looked like a victim of a shipwreck. He was half-naked and emaciated; his skin, wrinkled by long immersion in water, was sunburned and raw. When the townspeople carried him to shore, the words that came from his cracked lips were incoherent; his blood-shot eyes, flickering back and forth beneath the matted hair on his forehead, were like those of a terrified animal. Several days passed before he recovered enough to tell his Mormon benefactors what he had been through. This man —James White— told a story what would be argued about for years to come.

White was a prospector, a simple, roughshod frontiersman hoping to get lucky in the wild, unexplored country between the San Juan Mountains and the Colorado River. His luck, he admitted to the good folks of Callville, was nothing but bad. He told them his incredible tale, and then carefully penned a letter to his brother in Wisconsin. James White was barely literate, so his letter is a curious thing to read. But it was accepted by many as proof that he actually did ride through the Grand Canyon, since his brother, Josh White, swore James would never lie to him.

"Dear Brother," James White wrote. "i went prospected with Captin Baker and gorge strole in the San Won montin Wee found vry god prospect but noth that wold pay then Wee cross over on Coloreado and Camp..."

This jumble of words matched White's verbal account of the start of his odyssey. He and two companions, Captain Baker and George Strole, had followed the San Juan River for what he thought was about 200 miles over a period of three weeks. Upon reaching the Colorado River, they pitched camp at the top of a side canyon. Which canyon it was has never been determined, but it undoubtedly would be in the Glen Canyon area.

"Wee lad over one day," White continued in his letter. "Wee found out that Wee cold not travel down the river and our hourse Was Sore fite Wee made up our mines to turene back When Wee was attacked by 15 or 20 indis they killed Baker and then gorge strole and myself tok fore ropes off from our hourse and a axe ten pounds of flour and our gunns Wee had 15 millse to woak to Coloreado Wee got to the river Jest at night..."

Fearful that the Indians might still be pursuing them, White and Strole quickly built a raft by tying three cottonwood logs together with their ropes. The raft was ten feet long and barely two feet wide, but the two men quickly straddled it and pushed off into the dark, rushing waters.

"We had good sailing for three days and the fore day gorge strole was wash off from the raft and drown that left me alone i thought that it would be my time next i then pool off my boos and pands i then tide a rope to my wase i wend over falls from 10 to 15 feet hie my raft Wold tip over three and fore times a day..."

Each night, White would tie his raft to riverside rocks and sleep on it for fear of losing it. His soggy sack of flour had been swept away during the first few days, so his only food was the few mesquite beans he was able to pick and a couple of lizards he was able to catch. By the end of the first week, White was so hungry he cut his leather knife scabbard into tiny pieces and swallowed them. In one of the more violent rapids, the raft broke apart. White spread-eagled himself over the logs and held them together until they plowed into a sandbar. He somehow managed to untangle the ropes, re-tie the original logs, add a few more, and shove off again.

On the thirteenth day, White came across a "party of indis freney they Wold not give me noth to eat so i give my pistols for hine pards of a dog i ead one for super and the other breakfast the 14 day i rive at Callville Whare i Was tak Care of i was ten days With out pands or boos or hat i Was soon bornt so i Cold hadly woak Joosh i Can rite yu thalfe i under Went i see the hardes time that eny man ever did in the World but thatk god that i got thught saft i am Well a gin and i hope the few lines Will fine yu all Well i sned my beck respeck to all Joosh ance this when yu git it James White."

White posted his laboriously written letter and resumed his life as a ne'er-do-well drifter. His story was told frequently by the folks in and around Callville, but it did not attract much attention outside that area until Powell's expedition made its successful run through the Grand Canyon. When the newspapers heralded Powell's accomplishment, Josh White took his brother's letter to the press. It was published, usually with the spelling corrected, in several major newspapers. A journalist from the *Rocky Mountain News* in Denver located James White in Trinidad, Colorado, where he conducted a lengthy interview with the old prospector. White stuck to his original story, but admitted he didn't know exactly where he entered the canyon or precisely how many days he traveled down the Colorado.

Powell, naturally, scoffed at the story when he heard it. He said he knew from personal experience that no man could possibly survive if he tried to run the river in the manner White described. White, according to Powell, was "a monumental prevaricator, the biggest liar that ever told a tale about the Colorado River."

Still, White had definitely come out of the canyon, and he had obviously been in it for a number of days. The real question seemed to be: did he travel the full length of the canyon or only a portion of it? Powell insisted that under no circumstances could the voyage be accomplished in two weeks; after all, it had taken his group 27 days, and they were experienced and well-equipped. White's defenders countered by pointing out that White spent all his time plummeting downstream, hanging on for dear life; he did not take time out for explorations of side canyons or for collecting scientific data.

The controversy simply could not be resolved; White's account could neither be verified nor disproved. However, it was an undisputed fact that Powell did make it down the entire length of the Colorado, and the vast majority of the general public accepted him and his comrades as the first to conquer the Grand Canyon. After the canyon was granted National Park status in 1919, a monument was erected on West Rim Drive, near El Tovar Hotel, to commemorate this outstanding achievement. By that time, James White had died in obscurity.

But a new controversy over Powell's "first" arose several years later. In 1932, Herbert Gregory, a professor at the University of Utah, announced he had discovered the identify of someone who may well have gone through the Grand Canyon 30 years ahead of both Powell and White.

During the summer of 1931, Gregory had gone for a hike along Utah's Uintah River. On a bluff above the river, there is a vertical sandstone slab commonly referred to as Fur Traders' Rock. Here, during the Mountain Man era of the 1830s, many trappers and hunters had carved their names on the stone before they wandered on. As a historian, Gregory had always wanted to see the rock, to record the names and dates inscribed on it. But when he finally walked up to the stone, he was quite surprised by what he saw.

One name in particular caught his eye. "I'll be damned," he said, as he traced his fingers over the letters. "Denis Julien. So *that* was his first name. Well, Mr. Denis Julien, you and I are going to have to get better acquainted."

Professor Gregory was familiar with the name D. Julien, for it had been mentioned in two of the books written by early explorers of the Grand Canyon. Frederick Dellenbaugh, a member of Powell's second expedition through the canyon in 1872, reported having seen the name carved on a rock in Labyrinth Canyon near the river. It was dated 1836. Robert Brewster Stanton discovered D. Julien's signature twice while surveying the canyon in 1889 for the proposed, but completely preposterous, Colorado Canyon Railway. Two different parties of prospectors also told of seeing the name in two different locations, both close to the river.

The most interesting of these petroglyphs was the second one that Stanton found. It was high up on a sandstone wall beneath an overhanging cliff where it could only have been made by someone standing in a boat during fairly high water. D. Julien had carefully etched in his name, dated it "1836, 3 Mai." Beside his signature, he had drawn a picture of a boat with a mast. Below the boat was a very strange drawing; it appeared to be a winged sun, a fiery orb flying directly at the viewer. No one had been able to figure out what it represented.

Originally, it was assumed Julien had made several trips from the rim to the river during 1836, but when the drawing of the boat was discovered, it began to seem quite possible he was actually trying to travel down the river itself. Since none of his signatures had ever been found in the lower part of the canyon, he was believed to have perished in the attempt.

Who was this mysterious fellow? Professor Gregory decided to see if he could find out. Clearly, Denis Julien had been a fur trader. The date he scratched on the rock in Uintah Canyon was 1831, and there was a thriving fur trade in the upper Colorado Basin at that time. Gregory contacted the Missouri Historical Library in St. Louis to ask if there was any information on Denis Julien in the library's extensive collection of records on Nineteenth Century French traders. The library soon confirmed that there certainly were such records.

Julien had been a French-Canadian who migrated to Louisiana in the late 1700s. Baptismal records show his three children were born there in the 1790s. After his children were grown, he traveled west and went to work for Antoine Robidoux's fur company in Utah in 1831.

The intrigued professor then made inquiries locally in the Uintah River area and learned that several other hikers had also seen D. Julien's signature in a variety of places. One carving, located below the junction of the Green and Grand Rivers, was dated 1844. Gregory was elated at this news. It proved Denis Julien did not die in the Grand Canyon in 1836, and it raised the possibility that he must have made it all the way through. But, as in the case of James White, it can never be proven.

If either White or Julien did actually run the river ahead of Powell, it does not detract from Powell's magnificent accomplishment. He and his intrepid crew had "ridden the dragon" and come out alive. Then, three years later, they went back and did it all over again.

By the same token, Powell's adventures take no glory away from those who followed him.

In 1937, Haldane Holmstrom made the first officially acknowledged solo run of the river, following Powell's route from Green River, Wyoming to Boulder Dam. At this time, it was still firmly, but quite mistakenly, believed that river-running in the Grand Canyon was strictly a male undertaking. If stout-hearted men could barely live through the experience, it certainly was beyond the capabilities of a woman, it was thought. But in 1938, Dr. Elzada Clover and Lois Jotter wiped out that theory when they became the first women to successfully raft down the canyon.

Seven years later, Georgie White and Harry Aleson pulled off an incredibly daring stunt by swimming the length of the Grand Canyon in life jackets. White apparently enjoyed being tossed about like a human cork so much that she repeated the trip a few years later. Beyond any doubt, Georgie White is the all-time champion Colorado river-runner; over a period of more than 30 years, she virtually lived on the river, running commercial excursions and introducing the innovative boating techniques (such as the three-raft G-Rig) that have made possible the safe but still exhilarating voyages of the present day.

A raft trip through the Grand Canyon is joyous and immensely rewarding, but it should be remembered that, until fairly recently, a Colorado River run could be a fatal encounter with a merciless river of no return. Over the years, a disturbing number of people who entered the canyon did not come out the other end. To die in the Grand Canyon is to die a lonely death, to vanish under circumstances that will forever remain mysterious.

One of the most horrific Colorado River deaths was discovered by Stanton's expedition in June 1889. A skeleton was found crushed inside the wreckage of a wooden wagon more than 150 miles downstream from the nearest possible river crossing. Stanton surmised that someone had misjudged the depth of the Colorado and attempted to ford it. Just as likely, the wagon simply got too close to the river just as a flash flood unleashed the Colorado's full fury. Either way, the thought of a team of terrified, neighing horses disappearing into a seething caldron as the wagon turned over and over behind them is a nightmarish image.

Even the veteran river runners of that glorious early era never knew when the river would decide to take them under. Albert "Bert" Loper's disappearance is probably the classic example. Bert Loper seemed to have been destined from birth to devote his life to the Colorado River. He eventually gave it both body and soul.

Loper was born on July 31, 1869, the exact day that Powell and his audacious crew fought their way out of the rapids in Cataract Canyon. In 1893-94, Loper frequently ran the San Juan River as a prospector, but it was not until 1907 that he took a shot at the Colorado. During that summer, he and two companions set forth in three steel boats. The first boat was wrecked in Cataract Canyon; the second was destroyed by the Hance Rapid, 76 miles into the Grand Canyon; the third was so severely damaged by Hermit Rapid, 18 miles on down, that it is a miracle the boat made it the rest of the way down. Loper's friends thought the trip was miserable and terrifying, but Loper felt it was the most thrilling experience of his life. From that time on, he was totally addicted to river running.

Bert Loper ran the river again and again, often solo. He became a guide and chief boatman for several scientific expeditions. Over a period of 40 years, he earned the title "Grand Old Man of the Colorado." By 1949, his eightieth birthday approaching, he decided to celebrate by going down his beloved river one last time.

He knew it would be his final run. His health was failing, and his heart was telling him it wouldn't be pumping much longer. He pushed off from Lee's Ferry on July 7, during the eightieth anniversary summer of the Powell expedition. He planned to emerge from the canyon on July 31. Loper was accompanied by a passenger, Wayne Nichol, two other boats, and a neoprene raft. The next day, Unnamed Rapid upset his boat and Bert Loper was last seen swirling away ahead of it.

Nichol, the passenger, made it to shore and joined the others in a desperate search for the old man. His capsized boat was found jammed into the rocks 17 miles from the site of the accident, but Loper was gone for good. Twenty-six years passed before a hiker stumbled across a few of his bones in 1975. Ironically, they had washed ashore just below Lava Falls Rapid. Bert Loper, even though he was dead, had made it through that devilish plunge one last time.

After the bones were positively identified as those of a toothless, 80-year-old man of the same height as Bert, they were buried beside his wife's grave in Sandy, Utah. Bert's remains are gone from the Grand Canyon, but plenty of folks claim his spirit is still there. They swear he has often been seen gliding along in his ghostly boat in the middle of the night. And, of course, whenever a camper's coffee pot suddenly overturns, or a piece of equipment is mysteriously lost, Old Bert always gets the blame.

Perhaps the saddest, most poignant river tragedy was the one that occurred in 1928. In October that year, a pair of young honeymooners, Glen and Bessie Hyde, came hiking up from the river on the Bright Angel Trail. They knocked on the door of the Kolb brothers' photographic studio which, at that time, was located at the trailhead.

Emory and Ellsworth Kolb were the foremost Grand Canyon photographers of their day. From 1901 to 1941, they captured the canyon's grandeur as no other photographers had. The Kolbs had once even attempted to film a cops-and-robbers movie in the canyon featuring a climactic scene in which the good guys chase the bad guys through the rapids. The actors survived the chase scene, but the camera did not; it was submerged and the film was ruined. Eventually, the Kolbs did manage to film a rather impressive documentary about the canyon and for many years, they showed it to the tourists who visited their studio.

The Kolbs had built their combination studio and residence into the side of the cliff so that the first floor was below the rim and the second floor above it. Along side this vertical log cabin, they posted a large sign which read: "Bright Angel Toll Road. Riding Animals. Pack Animals. Loose Animals. $1.00 each." By 1928, a steady stream of tourists was handing one-dollar bills to the Kolb brothers for the privilege of straddling burros rented from the nearby stables for a trip into the world's most glorious gully. The Kolbs kept pretty close track of everyone who came and went on Bright Angel Trail, so they were somewhat surprised when this young couple hiked in from below.

After the Hydes had introduced themselves, they explained they were spending their honeymoon rafting through the canyon. They had been on the river for 26 days, and expected to conclude their journey within a week or two. But now, they wished to have their picture taken standing together on the rim of the Grand Canyon. Emory Kolb said he would be more than happy to do so.

As he was setting up his camera, Kolb asked them a little about themselves. The Hydes, he learned, were from Idaho, where Glen Hyde had occasionally run that state's wild rivers. He was tall and strong, with an air of self-confidence. Bessie, by contrast, was a small woman. She stood only to her husband's shoulder; Kolb guessed she didn't weigh much more than 90 pounds. He studied her face closely. There was something about her eyes that bothered him; he felt he saw a look of fear. He asked them about their boat.

"Built her ourselves," Glen said proudly. "Twenty-foot scow with sweep oars on both ends. She's a good one, all right."

"And, of course, you wear life preservers?"

"Nope," Glen Hyde answered. "Don't need 'em."

Kolb was incredulous. "My God," he exclaimed. "You really should have life preservers. I'll loan you a couple of mine."

Glen shook his head. There was a touch of bravado in his voice as he said, "No thanks. Powell's bunch made it through without life jackets. And so will we."

Kolb glanced over at Bessie, but she averted her eyes. "How you been managing the rapids?" he asked Glen. "Been going ashore and lining your boat past them with ropes?"

"Couple of times," the young husband replied. "But usually when we hear one coming up, we bank the boat and my Bessie holds her there with a rope. I walk downstream, size up the rapid and, after I've seen what's coming next, we shoot right through."

Now Bessie Hyde spoke up. "Glen's been thrown out of the boat twice," she said softly. "Once in Sockdolager Rapid and once in..."

"Well, that is true," her husband interrupted. "But each time, my Bessie threw me a rope and I got right back on board."

Kolb shuddered. "I sure hope your luck continues to hold up," he said. "Well, give me a big smile." He peered through his camera lens and clicked the shutter.

"Thank you, Mr. Kolb," said Glen Hyde. "We'll be looking forward to seeing that picture when we come back. Now, Bessie, my girl, we'd best be getting back down that trail."

Bessie Hyde hesitated only a moment before saying, "Yes, I suppose we should." Emory Kolb frowned. "She *really* doesn't want to go back to that river," he thought.

By now, Kolb's daughter, Emily, had come out of the studio to greet the young couple. As always, Emily Kolb was primly and neatly dressed. The two women smiled at one another. Bessie Hyde, speaking almost as if she were talking to herself, said, "I wonder if I shall ever wear pretty shoes again." Then, she turned and followed her husband down Bright Angel Trail.

The date was November 16. Neither Emory nor Emily Kolb slept well that night; they both kept thinking of Bessie Hyde's parting words. The days went by and turned into weeks. By early December, there was still no sign of the Hydes. "I don't think they made it, Daddy," said Emily. Her father agreed. He initiated a

search which included a small airplane sent out from
March Air Base to fly through the inner gorge. It was
the first time such a flight had ever been attempted.
The pilot soon spotted the Hyde's blunt-nosed scow
snagged in the rocks 14 miles below Diamond Creek.

Emory Kolb joined the rescue party that hiked
down from the rim. When they reached the boat, they
found everything intact and carefully secured; food,
clothing, even books were neatly in place. A long rope
was floating out ahead of the scow, indicating it was in
use at the time of the accident. Though the rescuers
made a long and thorough search, no trace of Glen or
Bessie Hyde was ever found.

The last rapid that the boat passed through is
called 232 Mile Rapid, and it is a mean one. Below
232, there are only two more rapids to run before
reaching smooth water. The Hydes almost made it. If
they had, Bessie Hyde would have earned the honor of
being the first woman to make a river run through the
Grand Canyon.

What happened to them?

Were they on the shore trying to line the scow
past the rapid, only to be pulled into deadly current?
Or was the diminutive Bessie braced in the rocks with
the rope around her tiny waist, holding the boat
against the current while Glen walked ahead to take a
look at the next furious burst of white water? Was she
jerked into the river, and did Glen dive in to try and
save her? These questions will never be answered for
only the river knows what befell the ill-fated couple.

More than 60 years have passed since the Hydes
disappeared; more than 120 years since Powell's tri-
umph. Four and a half centuries have gone by since
the first Spanish explorers stood on the rim. Yet, all
this time was but a split-second in the lifetime of the

Grand Canyon. The era of human activity in the canyon, though it has been dramatic, has been very brief. Nevertheless, humanity's impact is comparable to that of a full geologic age. If Powell, D. Julien, James White or the Hydes could see their canyon today, they would undoubtedly be startled and dismayed.

The Grand Canyon's wild river is now confined between two massive dams which corral it like a still untamed bucking mustang. The widely fluctuating releases of water from Glen Canyon Dam cause the river level to rise and fall as much as 13 feet a day, creating continuous flash floods that are wiping out the beaches, sandbars, marshes and delicate riparian wildlife habitat. Power plant smog drifts over the canyon in such density that sometimes the north rim cannot be seen from the south.

But the Colorado rolls on, unmindful of these temporary annoyances. It is busily filling up the dam's reservoirs with silt and fossilizing the bones of its human victims just as it encased its prehistoric inhabitants in limestone hundreds of millions of years ago. And it is slowly digging its way deeper into the earth's crust. To the canyon, human intrusions have been little more than subliminal flashes in its eons of existence. But the brave men and women who dared to enter the Grand Canyon when it was still an unknown realm certainly never forgot their adventures. The exploratory era lasted only for a moment, but what a glorious moment it was.

How to Run the Colorado River

A list of 212 river-running concessionaires currently operating in the Grand Canyon is available from Grand Canyon National Park, P.O. Box 129, Grand Canyon AZ 86023.

Trips vary from one to 14 days, depending on the distance covered. Most trips begin at Lee's Ferry, while others depart from points which can be reached only by trail. The river is run year-round, but most excursions are launched between April and October. The river companies provide food, portable sanitation facilities, camping items and guide services. Both motorized and oar-powered voyages are offered. Consequently, a wide range of prices is offered. Shop around for the trip that suits you best; make reservations well in advance.

Bibliography - Chapter 7

Babbit, Bruce. **Grand Canyon, An Anthology.** Flagstaff, Arizona, North Land Press. 1978.

Corle, Edwin. **Listen, Bright Angel.** New York. Duell, Sloan and Pearce. 1946.

Evans, Edna. **Tales from the Grand Canyon.** Flagstaff, Arizona, North Land Press. 1985.

Lavender, David. **Colorado River Country.** New York. E.P. Dutton, Inc. 1946.

McAdams, Cliff. **Grand Canyon National Park Guide and Reference Book.** Boulder, Colorado. Pruett Publishing Company. 1981.

Powell, John Wesley. **Canyons of the Colorado.** Meadeville, Pennsylvania. Flood & Finch. 1895. Reprinted as **Explorations of the Colorado and its Canyons.** New York. Dover. 1961.

Wisenberg, Dinah. *Congressional Quarterly.* Washington, D.C. August, 1990.

8

The Last of the
Mystic Lone Wolves

Surely the most enigmatic beasts ever to roam the Southwest were the wild, lone wolves of yesteryear. For more than half a century, these phantom-like rogues, these solitary survivors of once-large packs, prowled the range lands of southern Arizona and northern Mexico, preying on ranchers' livestock while outwitting all pursuers.

The lone wolves were so elusive, so skilled at sur-

vival that many ranchers on both sides of the border
swore there had to be something supernatural about
them. It just didn't seem possible that ordinary flesh-
and-blood animals could travel so freely and kill with
such impunity while half the hunters in Arizona and
Chihuahua were on their trails.

Anyone who has ever heard the eerie howl of a
wolf can understand these ranchers' superstitious
beliefs. Throughout the ages, humans and animals
alike have frozen in their tracks and glanced fearfully
into the darkness when this mysterious beast lets out
its terrifying wail. When a wolf howls, all other sounds
go unheard.

The great conservationist Aldo Leopold once
described the howl as "a deep chesty bawl that echoes
from rimrock to rimrock, rolls down the mountain, and
fades into the far blackness of the night. It is an outburst of wild defiant sorrow, and of contempt for all the
adversities of the world. It tingles in the spine of all
who hear wolves by night, or who scan their tracks by
day."

The fear of wolves runs deep in the human psy-
che. It is a primordial fear, an angst dating back to the
earliest of times when humans huddled together in
mortal dread of the non-human creatures lurking just
beyond the glow of the campfire. In part, this fear
stems from the fact that wolves seem disturbingly similar to humans in many ways. They are highly intelli-
gent, cunning and crafty. They survive by outsmarting
their enemies, and they kill to get what they want.

Throughout history, mankind has tried by every
means possible to eradicate these fierce predators.
Until fairly recently, human beings have never passed
up an opportunity to kill a wolf. Even Aldo Leopold
once shot one. He later wrote: "I was young then and

full of trigger-itch." After he gunned down the wolf, he reached her while she was still alive, getting there just in time to watch the "green fire dying in her eyes." From that moment on Leopold could never bring himself to shoot another wolf.

The eyes of a wolf probably reveal more about this strange animal than its howl. Rimmed by semi-circles of black hair, they stare with that disturbing intensity seen only in the eyes of predators. Though a wolf's eyes narrow during an attack, its gaze is otherwise almost always wide, steady and mesmerizing. It is a look of pure wildness.

Many contemporary observers of wolves contend these animals possess extrasensory perception. How else can one explain the wolf's ability to avoid traps it cannot see or smell and elude hunters whose presence is so distant that they cannot be sighted? People who have raised wolves in captivity note that the animals often seem able to anticipate the arrival of their owner, can sense what a handler is going to do next, and can read peoples' moods, feelings and attitudes toward them.

Roy T. McBride, a wolf trapper who worked in Arizona and Mexico in the 1960s, once told of an experience he had on a ranch near Casas Grandes in Chihuahua. Two wolves were held captive on the ranch, chained in dusty neglect near the main house. They had been captured as pups and were being kept alive primarily as novelties. Even though he was a professional killer of wolves, McBride took pity on these pathetic, half-starved creatures. He began bringing back for the caged wolves any non-bounty animals (such as javelinas, coyotes and bobcats) accidentally caught in his traps. The two hungry lobos gratefully devoured those carcasses that would have been dis-

carded. Not surprisingly, the wolves took a strong lik-
ing to Roy T. McBride, and eagerly looked forward to
his occasional visits. The vaqueros who worked on the
ranch told McBride they could always tell when he was
going to show up, because the wolves would start to
bark and howl, running in circles. Then 20 minutes
later, the ranch dogs would begin to bark, and shortly
after that, McBride and his horse would be seen on the
horizon.

The wolf's highly evolved nature has enabled it to
survive and flourish in some of the world's most harsh
environments. Traditionally, wolves traveled in packs
which were tightly organized social units, similar in
many respects to bands of human hunters in prehistoric times. Each member of the pack, from the leader
—the alpha wolf— to the smallest and weakest pup
knew his or her place in this strict hierarchy. Through
a complicated system of dominance and submission,
cooperation and shared responsibilities, the wolves
thrived until modern times.

Wolf packs varied in size from four to 25 animals.
They practiced birth control, for they instinctively knew
that an effective pack could sustain itself only within
certain numbers. If times were lean, only the alpha
female would breed during the mating season, and
then give birth to a small litter. But in years when
game was plentiful, several females would breed and,
amazingly, produce large litters, sometimes as many as
nine pups.

After the pups were weaned, the other pack
members helped with the feeding by regurgitating partially digested food for them. Often, the pack cared for
its elderly as well. Old wolves who were no longer able
to take part in attacks were nonetheless allowed a
share of the kill. Presumably the elders' experience in

locating prey was still valued by the younger wolves.

But the wolf's world was usually feast-or-famine. It was not uncommon for a wolf to go several days without eating. Then, after a kill, it might gorge itself on as much as 20 pounds of meat in a single meal.

In their extraordinary wisdom, wolves usually practiced a sort of conservation ethic. Like wise farmers who leave fields fallow for a few years to allow the land to recover its growing capacity, wolves ordinarily departed their hunting grounds before the prey population was depleted. There were exceptions, however. At times, wolves were known to kill much more game than they needed for food. Perhaps during the frenzied excitement of the chase and attack, they completely lost control to the killer instinct, unable to cease the slaughter once it began. If so, this kind of ferocity can be readily understood by human beings. Some ethnologists have suggested that mankind might have learned more about the origins of its own basic nature by studying wolves, rather than primates.

All in all, the wolves' predations may have done more good than harm. By culling the deer herds, they prevented overgrazing in their habitat. And, by killing more than they could eat, they inadvertantly fed a host of other species. Coyotes, foxes, bobcats, bears and a wide variety of birds dined well on the wolves's leavings. Often carnivorous animals would follow wolf packs, knowing that, if they were patient, dinner would be served.

A very special member of the wolves' entourage was the raven. Some naturalists swear there was actually a close bond between these sagacious birds and the wolves. Reportedly, ravens would fly ahead of the wolf packs to locate game, and then come winging back to lead the wolves to their prey. Further evidence of this strange raven-wolf affinity comes from the fact that, of all the non-canine species, wolves would allow themselves to be teased only by ravens. Ravens have been seen making sudden, wing-flapping, dive-bombing attacks on the heads of sleeping wolves. Observers have seen ravens waddle up quietly behind a wolf and pull its tail. One wolf's response to these pranks was to go into a hunting crouch, make a slow, exaggerated approach toward the winged practical joker, and jump playfully just as the bird flew away in mock fright. Apparently, these odd partners-in-crime had a great sense of humor.

Wild wolves of yesteryear were very territorial. They claimed vast areas as their domain and subtly but clearly defined their boundaries and runways with urine on bushes and scratch marks in the dirt. Trespassers from neighboring packs were dealt with severely; fights to defend a pack's chosen hunting grounds and denning sites were often fights to the death.

During the wolves's heyday, 20 to 30 subspecies existed worldwide. The primary wolf of Arizona was known as *canis lupis baileyi*, or, more commonly, the Mexican gray wolf. They ranged from northern Mexico on up through Arizona, New Mexico and western Colorado. Their runways, or travel circuits, followed the arroyos, washes and trails in an intricate network of hundreds of miles of hunting paths.

Although never as abundant as other predators in Arizona, the Mexican gray wolves were the undisputed rulers of their domain. For centuries they had no real competition. But when human settlers came, everything changed.

As two-legged predators arrived in increasing numbers, wild game grew scarce. The wolves' traditional food sources dwindled. Ironically, the people killing off the indigenous wildlife replaced it with dumber, slower-moving prey for wolves. Antelope grasslands were turned into sheep pastures, deer habitat became cattle ranges, and the wolves helped themselves. But this forced change in diet eventually brought them to the brink of extinction.

Financial losses suffered by ranchers due to wolf predation were never as great as those caused by over-grazing and drought, but they were serious nonetheless, particularly on the smaller ranches where the loss of just a few cattle or sheep could be disastrous. Ranchers fought back with rifles, steel traps and poisoned baits. The wolves, in turn, defended themselves by learning to run at the sight of a rifle, to detect and avoid the terrible toothed jaws of the hidden traps and to urinate contemptuously on the enticing baits.

By the end of the Nineteenth Century, Arizona ranchers realized they could not win their war against the wolves without government assistance. In 1893 they lobbied the Arizona-New Mexico Territorial Legislature into passing the Territorial Bounty Act which allowed county officials to appropriate money to pay bounties on predators. That put the hunting of wolves into the hands of professionals who killed hundreds of wolves in the next two decades.

As the once-mighty packs grew fewer and smaller, a new chapter in the history of Arizona wolves began, a chapter filled with nearly unbelievable tales of animal cunning. This was the era of the lone wolves.

Many of these rogues were survivors of decimated packs, but others may have sensed that it was suicidal to stay with a pack and therefore gone off on their own. Possibly, like some humans, they simply knew they were born to be outlaws. Just as Jesse James and Billy the Kid enjoyed larger-than-life reputations for their daring exploits, so did the lone wolves.

The trail of slaughter by these loners tended to become exaggerated as the stories spread from one ranch to the next, but the damage was undeniably extensive. One had to take with a grain of salt reports that a single wolf had killed an entire herd of cattle or flock of sheep overnight, but when a round-up crew of cowboys rode out at the end of summer to bring in the herd they had turned loose in the spring, only to find mostly bones and carcasses, it was clear that something terribly ferocious had been on the prowl.

Hunters were awed by these arrogant predators since they were so hard to track down and kill. Each lone wolf was given a name, so they developed status as living legends.

One of Arizona's most famous wolves was the Chiricahua Wolf, so called because he ranged in and around the Chricahua Mountains for several years.

This wolf had a sizable appetite. Allegedly he killed an average of one yearling every four days. Although this was definitely more than enough food for a single wolf, there was a good reason for the Chiricahua wolf's excesses; he was ambush-wise and much too smart to return to a carcass for a second meal. The Chiricahua wolf's luck finally ran out in the summer of 1916 when a professional "wolfer," A.W. Mills, managed to get him within the sights of his rifle.

A wolf named Old Aguila took up where the Chiricahua wolf left off. She began her eight-year reign of depredation in 1916. The name means "eagle" in Spanish. She must be able to fly, her perplexed pursuers reasoned; how else could she invariably escape encirclements by horsemen and hounds? Old Aguila was a white wolf, credited with slaughtering livestock worth so many thousands of dollars in Maricopa County that the bounty on her head was the highest ever: $500. Her prowess as a huntress was so great it was said that satellite bands of coyotes followed in her wake, getting fat from her leftovers. It was not until 1924 that another "wolfer" brought her down.

Then there was Old One Toe, another fabled lone wolf of the 1920s. During the early part of his predatory career, this big lobo lost three of his toes in a trap. After that unpleasant experience, he developed an uncanny knack for detecting even the most carefully hidden traps. Upon discovering one, he would use the claw of his single toe to scratch a line in the dirt pointing directly at it. He seemed to be saying:"Just how dumb do you think I am?"

Old One Toe reached a ripe old age before he finally grew careless enough to step into a set of powerful steel jaws a second and final time.

All of the old-time lone wolves were fantastic creatures that stirred the imaginations of their human enemies. But the greatest rogue of all was, surprisingly, a contemporary wolf, an almost mystical renegade who roamed and plundered Arizona and northern Mexico in the 1960s.

By that time, the days of the Mexican gray wolf were all but over. The federally-funded Predatory Animal and Rodent Control (PARC) service had, during a period of more than 40 years, been very successful. In addition to using traps and hunting rifles, PARC employed powerful chemical canicides such as strychnine, arsenic and the deadly Compound 1080. Dens were dug up so the pups could be killed before they matured. Adult wolves were chased by airplane and shot from the air. It took a mighty smart wolf to survive under those conditions. One of the few that did was Las Margaritas.

A three-toed wolf, Las Margaritas always left a distinctive track at the site of each of his kills. But no one could follow that unmistakeable track for any distance. Once he had eaten his fill, he simply trotted off and vanished. His runways traversed the wildest, most inaccessible parts of the 250-mile stretch of deserts and mountains that sprawl out between the heart of Chiricahua and southern Arizona. Las Margaritas knew his territory so well he rarely had to travel the same route twice. He might enter a pasture by a rut road and leave by a game trail. By the time a hunter could locate the exit route, the savvy wolf was many miles away.

This unstoppable rogue began his killing spree in the late 1950s on the Rancho de Las Margaritas near Durango, Mexico. For nearly a decade, he killed an estimated 100 steers, cows and calves each year, and outwitted scores of angry pursuers. Most of the wolfers eventually came to the frustrating conclusion that they were wasting their time trying to bring this one down. After ten years of setting traps, they had only been able to take off one toe from this fabled beast.

Then in 1968, after everyone else had pretty much given up on trying to capture Las Margaritas, Roy T. McBride decided to take him on. McBride's reputation as a wolf hunter was almost as big as Las Margaritas' fame. He was probably the best wolfer of his day and Las Margaritas represented the big challenge.

McBride knew the secret of wolf hunting was to get ahead of the wolf, not to follow it. So the hunter had to figure out where the wolf would go next, and be ready when the lobo arrives. The hunter had to be able to think like an animal, and McBride was one of those rare individuals who seemed able to do that.

Las Margaritas spent most of his time in those

days prowling and killing on the ranches west of Ciudad Chihuahua. McBride carefully scouted this wild, desolate terrain and discovered several wolf runways. He chose the one he thought the stealthy rogue would most likely travel after his next raid. Then he prepared some very sophisticated poisoned baits.

Before he began, McBride tied a bandana over his face so he would not even breathe on the bait. He put on leather gloves soaked in cow's blood before cutting a calf's liver into chunks with a boiled knife blade. Into each piece of liver, he inserted capsules of cyanide and strychnine. He placed the deadly baits in a blood-smeared buckskin bag and dragged them behind his horse to the wolf runway. After dropping the baits at quarter-mile intervals, he rode back to his camp by another route. He settled down to wait.

He let a week go by before returning to pick up what he expected to be a dead wolf. Instead, he found that Las Margaritas had defecated on the first bait and loped on past the others without breaking stride.

Now McBride knew he was up against a truly worthy opponent. Even though Las Margaritas was far too clever to gulp down the poisoned hor d'oeuvres, the fanatical hunter firmly believed that no wolf had ever been born that could evade his diabolical traps. He rummaged through his huge collection of wolf-killing devices and pulled out his favorite trap: a bone-crushing, six-pound Newhouse #114 with a three-toothed steel jaw.

He boiled the trap in oak leaves before taking it to one of Las Margaritas' scent-stations, a juniper tree which the great rogue wolf periodically marked with urine. After stepping down from his horse onto a steer hide, McBride set the trap and covered it with carefully sifted dirt and dry leaves. It was perfectly concealed, but, three days later, he found Las Margaritas had approached the trap, scuffed dirt on it with his hind feet and gone on his way.

During the months that followed, the wolf trapper used every trick he knew. He set double traps — one which was poorly concealed next to a second which was perfectly hidden. The idea, of course, was that the wolf would step around the first trap and be caught by the second. Las Margaritas wasn't fooled for a moment. He cautiously skirted both.

Frequently McBride used "blind-sets," traps set in strategic places where a wolf could not avoid stepping on them. For example, he once placed a trap on the other side of a pine tree that had fallen across a cow trail, positioning it so the wolf would land on it when he jumped over the log. McBride probably wasn't even surprised when he later found Las Margaritas' tracks stopped at the log, detoured around it, and kept going.

By then, McBride had been on Las Margaritas' trail for almost a full year. He was beginning to agree with the ranchers: this animal *was* supernatural. It was a wraith, not a wolf. Then one day McBride got an idea. It suddenly dawned on him that he might have been overlooking this shrewd beast's one and only weakness. He remembered that Las Margaritas almost always stopped to sniff campfire ashes when he came across them. Probably, he was curious about the strange foods that humans cooked there.

"Maybe," McBride thought, "Just maybe, your curiosity about us two-legged critters will be your downfall." Putting his plan into action, he set his trusty, old Newhouse #114 beside a trail near a pasture, built a wood fire over it and let it burn down to ashes. Then he tossed a small amount of bacon scraps and grease alongside it. "Breakfast is served," he said. "Come and get it."

In less than a week, Las Margaritas took his last step as a free animal. McBride was waiting several miles away, so he could not have heard the great lobo's sudden "outburst of wild, defiant sorrow" when the trap's fanged jaws flashed out of the ashes and seized his foot. Without hearing it, McBride somehow sensed the trap had been sprung. He saddled up and rode over. For the first time, the two legendary hunters came face to face.

Usually when a trapper approaches a trapped wolf, the frantic beast will go wild, lunge and pull in a pain-crazed, hopeless attempt to rip itself free. Las Margaritas just stood there, staring McBride straight in the eyes. For one long moment, the man and the wolf looked at one another. Then McBride drew his rifle from its scabbard and fired a single bullet through Las Margaritas' wild heart.

The great wolf's hunting days were over —but so were McBride's. There were now virtually no wolves left to hunt anywhere in the Southwest. In 1970, one wolf was poisoned in New Mexico's Peloncillo Mountains, two were shot by deer hunters in southwestern Texas and, in 1976, a protected wolf named Aravaipa was gunned down in a southern Arizona canyon owned by Defenders of Wildlife. This illegal act was believed by nearly everyone —hunters, stockmen and conservationiss alike— to have eliminated the very last free wolf in the state. Now everyone was sure the deep, chesty howl of a wolf would never again "echo from rimrock to rimrock, roll down the mountain, and fade into the blackness of the night."

But they were wrong; wild wolves were not yet totally extinct in Arizona. Out of the thousands that once ran so freely, there was still one pair of wild lobos left alive. The story of the last two survivors of the government-approved extermination campaign is truly one of the most remarkable tales in the annals of wolf lore.

The story began in the late 1960s, approximately the same time that McBride was stalking Las Margaritas. The locale was the Singing Valley Ranch near the edge of the Santa Rita Mountains. The ranch was home to Bill and Penny Porter and their three-year-old daughter, Becky. The ranch was fairly remote, so, for little Becky, it was sometimes a lonely place. She had no other children to play with. After the old family dog died, she had no pets. Still, she was a happy, cheerful child with a rich imagination. Her mother was not really surprised when Becky came bouncing into the home one day to announce she had found herself a doggie.

Penny Porter smiled indulgently as her daughter described the beautiful, *very* big dog she had discovered in the mesquite thickets beyond the ranch house. Penny was sure this was just another charming childhood fantasy until Becky grew very serious in pleading for her mom's help in caring for the new-found pet. "My doggie needs help, Mommie. He's hurt. He can't get up. I gave him lots of water, but he's still thirsty. Come with me, Mommie. Please."

Puzzled and now vaguely alarmed, the young mother followed her out through the screen door and watched her run swiftly into the scraggly brush. She lost sight of Becky momentarily in the dense thicket, but when she caught up with the child, she froze in horror.

Her mouth went dry and the hand she was holding above her eyes to shield the noonday glare dropped limply to her side. Little Becky Porter was sitting on the ground hugging the neck of an enormous Mexican gray wolf.

Resisting her instinctive impulse to rush forward and grab her daughter, Penny Porter took a slow tentative step toward the wolf. Instantly, the wolf's eyes narrowed and its mouth curled into a snarl. "No. No," Becky admonished her doggie. "You be good. That's my Mommie. She's going to help you." When she petted the wolf's coarse, scruffy head, the snarl disappeared. Penny could hardly believe her ears as she heard the thumping sound of a wagging tail.

The wolf was half in and half out of the hollow stump of a felled scrub oak. Penny could see only its head and shoulders, but she could tell there was something very wrong with the animal. It appeared to be extremely weak and sick. She remembered Becky talking about the wolf's thirst. As a ranch woman, Penny knew that unquenchable thirst accompanied the final agonies of wild animals dying of rabies. She knelt on the ground and held out her arms. In a voice barely above a whisper, she said, "Becky, come to Mommie."

The child pressed her face against the wolf's furry head and kissed his nose. "I'll be back," she promised. Then she ran to her mother who quickly picked her up and carried her as fast as she could out of the thicket, past the house and on to the corral where she found one of the ranch hands. "Jake," she called out. "Becky found a wolf down by the wash. I think it's got rabies."

Jake accompanied Penny back to the stump and bent down for a closer look at the wolf. "Phew!" he gagged with his hand over his nose. "That ain't rabies, Mrs. Porter. That's gangrene. This critter's hurt *real* bad. Be best if I just put him out of his misery." He started to walk back to the bunkhouse to get a rifle, but he met little Becky at the edge of the brush. Her brown eyes were wide with worry. "Can you make him well, Jake?" she asked. The ranch hand glanced at Penny. She sighed and smiled at her daughter, saying, "We'll try, honey."

Late that afternoon, Penny's husband, Bill, brought a veterinarian to the ranch to examine the wolf. The animal was visibly growing weaker; it offered no resistence when the vet deftly inserted a hypodermic needle between its shoulder blades. Within seconds, its massive head drooped onto its paws. "Gimme a hand now, Bill," the veterinarian said. "Let's pull him out of that stump and see what we got here. Boy, he's heavy, isn't he? About a hundred pounds, I'd say. Been shot twice through the hips. His bones are all busted up. Can't imagine how he made it down from the mountains to your ranch. Well, for your daughter's sake, let's hope it's not too late to patch him up."

The vet cut away the rotted flesh, dug out the splintered bones, cleansed the wounds with hydrogen-peroxide, and gave the wolf a penicillin shot. "I'll be back in the morning," he said as he closed his satchel. "I'm going to replace that hip bone with a metal rod. In the meantime, you tell Becky she better be thinking of a name for her new dog."

The little girl was delighted to learn her doggie was going to get well. She started thinking of a name. Had this wolf been named in the traditional way, he would have been labeled with the territory he inhabited, probably the Santa Rita wolf, or perhaps even Singing Valley wolf. But for reasons known only to her, Becky decided to call him Ralph.

Ralph's recovery was long and painful. For the first three months, he could barely drag himself around. At last he gained the strength to stand on all fours and take faltering steps. Once he learned to walk again. he became Becky's constant companion, limping along beside her wherever she went. Then, one spring day, Ralph disappeared. Becky was brokenhearted, but Jake consoled her. "It's mating season. Ralph's out there looking for a lady friend. Ain't likely he'll find one nowadays, so he'll be back. You wait and see."

Sure enough, a few weeks later, Ralph returned to resume his life at the Singing Valley Ranch. He did his best to earn his keep. Not only was he Becky's loyal friend and guardian, but he was also a very serious watch dog. The Porters noticed that not one coyote showed up at the ranch after Ralph marked his scent stations. When Becky was old enough to start school, Ralph accompanied her to the bus each morning and waited on the shoulder of the road until she returned in the afternoon.

Twelve years went by: Becky was 15 and Ralph could have been no younger. He was stiff and slow, but he still made his annual lonely journeys back to the wild. In 1981, he stayed away much longer than usual. When he finally staggered in, he was wounded again.

Bill Porter learned from a neighbor that some nearby ranchers had shot a large she-wolf the previous day and wounded her companion. So it appeared that Ralph had found a mate at last, only to lose her to a hunter's bullet. He would never find another, for there were no more wild wolves left other than himself.

Ralph's wound was not serious this time, so after he had been treated, he hobbled off into the night, back to the desert hills beyond Singing Valley. In the morning, he returned, rested throughout the day, and limped out again in the evening. Becky worried more about him now than ever before. She kept his food dish filled and always found it empty at daybreak, but Ralph kept growing thinner and weaker. At last, the inevitable day came when he did not come back.

Becky and Penny searched for him, combing the mesquite thickets and dry washes until they found him lying dead beside his old oak stump. Becky petted his shaggy head and wept. Then, from within the stump, came a soft whimper. Becky peered inside where two tiny yellow eyes blinked back at her. Scarcely able to believe what she was seeing, she reached into the hollow log and drew out a squirming little puppy.

Now she knew why Ralph had gone out every night since his mate was killed; she understood why he had grown so thin. He had been taking his food, carrying it in his stomach, to feed his motherless pup lying helpless somewhere in a distant den. As he grew steadily weaker, Ralph surely realized he would not be able to care for his offspring much longer on his own. So, he had lifted his precious puppy by the nape of the neck and carried it all the way to the old, hollow stump where he had lain down, totally exhausted, and died waiting for Becky.

The story of the life and death of Ralph reveals more about the true nature of these wondrous animals than all of the scare-stories passed down through the centuries. The wolf —demonized in both ancient fairy tales and modern paperback fictions— has never been fully understood. Now it probably never will be. There will never be another Ralph, a Chiricahua, or an Old Aguila. Their time has come and gone. If only everyone who once feared, hunted and hated the wolves had listened a little more closely to their bold howls and melancholy night-songs, they might not have been quite so eager to silence their wild voices.

How to Visit a Mexican Gray Wolf

An experimental reintroduction program for the gray wolf was begun in Arizona's Blue Range in 1998, but few people will ever see them in the wilderness. Two Mexican grays currently reside in the Navajo Nation Zoological and Botanical Park. Another calls the Arizona-Sonora Desert Museum home. In both cases, genetic studies of blood samples proved them to be pure wolf, with no dog inter-breeding.

The Arizona-Sonora Desert Museum is nestled in Tucson Mountain Park at 2021 North Kinney Road, 14 miles from downtown Tucson. From Interstate 10, take Speedway Boulevard or Ajo Way-Kinney Road west to the park. This living museum is open daily from 8:30 a.m. to 5 p.m. In addition to having an opportunity to stare into the beautiful, mysterious eyes of a wolf, you can observe many other animals, birds and plants native to the great Sonoran desert region.

Bibliography - Chapter 8

Brown, David E. **The Wolf in the Southwest: The Making of an Endangered Species.** Tucson. The University of Arizona Press.

Burbank, Jim. *New Mexico* magazine. Santa Fe. February, 1990.

Fox, Michael W. **Behavior of Wolves, Dogs and Related Canids.** Robert E. Krieger Publishing Company, Inc. Marabar, Florida. 1971.

Lawrence, R.D. **In Praise of Wolves.** Henry Holt and Company. New York. 1986.

Lopez, Barry Holstun. **Of Wolves and Men.** Charles Scribner's Sons. New York. 1978.

Porter, Penny. *Reader's Digest.* Pleasantville, N.Y. April 1984.

9

John Lee's Gold

Most lost treasure stories follow a dramatic, but familiar, three-part scenario. First, someone discovers a fabulous treasure. Next, through circumstances beyond that person's control, the treasure is lost. Then whole generations of searchers seek in vain to recover it.

But not all treasure stories fit this classic pattern. The tale of John Lee's gold has a more unusual story line. John Doyle Lee struck it rich in northern Arizona in the 1860s and stashed a substantial part of his gold in seven buckets somewhere in a remote desert canyon. After his death, the search began. The difference this time was that the treasure was rediscovered in an utterly improbable way —only to be lost a second and final time.

When John Lee originally came to the Southwest, he had no intention of becoming a prospector. He arrived in Utah in 1847 with the great migration of the

151

Church of the Latter Day Saints. Lee was a high-rank-
ing member of the Mormon hierarchy's inner circle.
Though not one of the 12 Elders, he was an officer in
the Mormon militia and one of the "adopted brothers"
of the Prophet Brigham Young.

In spite of his professed godliness, Lee was a
cruel and dastardly man, a cold-blooded villain destined to play a leading role in one of the most shocking
acts of savagery ever perpetrated in the American
Southwest.

The decade that followed the Mormon settlement
of the valleys around the Great Salt Lake was extremely turbulent. The Saints declared themselves to be
above the laws of the United States, swearing they
could only obey "Higher Laws" from God Himself as
revealed through the visions of their prophets.
Attempts by the federal government to install judges,
marshalls, a secretary of state and an Indian agent in
the territory were met with defiant rejection.

The Mormons' fervent desire for self-determina-
tion was so passionate that encounters with Gentiles
who dared enter this private desert kingdom were
becoming increasingly violent. In 1853, the federally
commissioned Gunnison survey team was ambushed
while exploring Utah's Great Basin for a transcontinental railroad route. John Gunnison and eight members
of his party were slain. The Mormon Church's dilatory
investigation of the atrocity dismissed it as an Indian
raid, but the four surveyors who survived by running
for their lives felt differently. They were sure the attacking riflemen were not Indians. And why, they asked,
would Indians steal the party's notebooks and maps?

The Gunnison massacre shocked the nation, but
it was only a prelude to a much more terrible slaughter
soon to come.

Late in the summer of 1857, an exceptionally large Gentile wagon train entered northern Utah. Led by Captain Alexander Fancher, the train was made up of more than 130 Methodist men, women, children and infants on their way to settle in California. The emigrants had equipped themselves well for their long journey from Arkansas. According to Arkansas State Senator William Mitchell, whose sons and their families were with the train, these pioneers had "about 40 wagons and several traveling carriages, at least 900 head of fine cattle, many valuable horses and mules, much household property, and a great deal of ready money."

Historical estimates vary as to the value of the wagon train, but the lowest figure available is $75,000.

As the train crossed Utah, it received a cold reception from the local Mormon residents. Fancher had hoped to buy food and supplies in Salt Lake City, but the town's merchants flatly refused to do business with him. So the wagons rolled on, south to a lush grassland known as Mountain Meadows. Here the weary Methodists set up camp and rested their animals for the next leg of their long journey. They had no way of knowing that in the nearby town of Cedar City, a group of grim-faced, dark-suited men had gathered to discuss a plot that would seal their fate and outrage the nation.

The Apostle George A. Smith had come down from Salt Lake City to inform the local church officials that "the wealth of these Gentiles is to be consecrated to the True Church." An evil scheme had been devised and John Lee was designated to carry it out. Lee was instructed to visit the Paiute villages in the area and to inflame the Indians' emotions with wild tales about the Fancher party. He was to tell them that these barbarous invaders shot Indians for sport; that they poi-

soned wells as they passed by. When the Indians had
been roused to a fury, Lee was to lead a huge war party
in an attack on the wagon train.

The surprise assault took place during the early
morning hours of Monday, September 6. John Lee, dis-
guised as an Indian, gave the order for 300 Paiute warriors to open fire from the high-ground positions above
the meadow which they had stealthily occupied during
the night. The initial barrage felled 23 emigrants, six or
seven of whom died instantly. The entire camp had
been caught completely off-guard. After the first frenzied minutes of shock and panic, the stunned pioneers
rallied to defend themselves. They dragged their wagons into a protective circle and, while their best marks-
men kept the attackers at a distance, they dug shallow
trenches, piling dirt in front of them. Within a few
hours, they had fortified their encampment, but their
situation was extremely desperate. They had very little
water and the nearest spring was more than 100 yards
away.

The Paiutes maintained their siege from Monday
to Thursday, when a large troop of Mormon militia
arrived at the site. This was the moment John Lee had
been waiting for. On Friday morning, September 11, he
removed his Indian disguise, put on his regular clothing, and marched down to the wagons with a white flag
in his hand.

Once Fancher admitted him into the encir-
clement, Lee told the terrified families who crowded
around him that he had come to save them. He said
that as soon as he got word of the ambush, he had
mobilized all the men he could find and ridden swiftly
to the rescue. He said he met immediately with Indian
leaders and learned they had been deceived by false
rumors of Methodist depredations. Fortunately, Lee

had calmed them down and arranged a ceasefire. The situation was still quite volatile, he said, but if certain conditions were met, he believed he and his men could escort everyone safely past the Indians.

Those conditions required that the Methodists hand over their guns and place themselves in the protective custody of the Mormons. Surely Alexander Fancher was somewhat suspicious of this fishy-sounding proposal, but what other choice did he have? He laid down his rifle and all the other emigrants did the same.

The unarmed men stepped warily out into the sunny meadow where a double-file of Lee's rifle-totting "protectors" awaited them. As the guards led the men away, the women and children emerged to follow them. The silent procession waded through the tall grass toward the base of a low hill upon which a gaunt, ornately uniformed man stood silhouetted against the sky. This man, Militia Major John Higbee, raised his arms and everyone stopped.

"Men of Zion!" Higbee shouted. "Do your duty!" Instantly, every male member of the Fancher wagon train was shot down.

Now the Paiutes swarmed out of their hiding places to butcher the women and children. John Lee joined in the slaughter: he stalked the killing field shouting, "O Lord, my God, receive their spirits!" as he shot the wounded with his pistol. After he killed a wounded woman, her two daughters jumped up and tried to run away. Lee pursued the girls, firing at them until he murdered both.

The Mountain Meadows Massacre was over in a matter of minutes; 121 men, women and children lay dead in the grass. Only 17 infants were spared. These babies were later adopted by Mormon families. All of

the Methodists' possessions were turned over to the
Saints' tithing office in Cedar City.

When news of the atrocity finally reached
Arkansas, the stunned relatives of the victims demanded to know what had happened. From Salt Lake City,
Brigham Young issued a report which laid the blame
entirely on the Indians. But before long rumors of the
non-Indian participation in the ghastly affair spread
beyond Utah. A team of federal investigators headed by
Justice John M. Cradelbaugh was dispatched to the
territory in early 1859. Realizing he would be a primary
suspect, Lee decided to make himself scarce; he soon
left Utah to settle in a remote part of Arizona. Although
John Lee had 18 wives, he took only his favorite,
Emma, with him. The two of them traveled to a distant
outpost on the Colorado River, appropriately named
Lonely Dell. Later, it would become known as Lee's
Ferry, since it was the only place where the river could
be crossed above the Grand Canyon.

John Lee established a ferry boat service which
earned him an adequate living by transporting the
occasional travelers back and forth across the Colorado. He and Emma also tended large vegetable
gardens and befriended a local 15-year-old, homeless
orphan named Robert Hilderbrand. No one who met
Lee during this tranquil period of his life ever suspected that this stern, but seemingly respectable man had
once been a mass murderer.

Lee was fascinated by the redrock maze of deep
canyons that surrounded Lonely Dell. What great
wealth, he wondered, might lie hidden in their unexplored shadows? He began spending much of his spare
time roaming the canyons, firm in his belief that if
there was gold to be found, God would lead him to it.
In the late 1860s, Lee's prayers were answered. He hit

paydirt somewhere north of the river.

At first, he shared his secret with no one; his years of living as a fugitive had made him cautious and furtive. But finally, he took Emma and the adopted son into his confidence. One night, after returning from the canyon country, he showed them a sack of nuggets which he then hid beneath Emma's bed. Shortly thereafter, he began taking the teenaged Hilderbrand with him on his trips. The route they followed was always the same: downriver for 12 or 15 miles to a grassy spot near Soap Creek Canyon. Here, Hilderbrand would pitch camp and stay with the horses while Lee went on alone. Within a couple of days, Lee would be back carrying a small sack of gold. On one occasion, he told Emma and the boy that he had a near-fortune hidden away in seven metal buckets... and there was plenty more where that came from. John Lee was steadily growing quite rich, but he was destined never to enjoy his wealth. His past was about to catch up with him.

Back in Utah, all efforts to get indictments in the Mountain Meadows Massacre case had been stymied by the territorial officials' refusal to cooperate with federal investigators. Then in 1874, Utah's self-proclaimed theocratic right to defy U.S. law was firmly taken away by an act of Congress. In June of that year, President Ulysses S. Grant signed legislation which established federal supremacy over the territory. He granted U.S. attorneys the authority to prosecute all criminal cases in the Mormon domain.

Armed with this authority, teams of U.S. marshalls set out to arrest the leaders of the massacre. But since all of these men were in hiding, it proved to be a near-impossible task. After several weeks of searching, the lawmen found and captured only one of the alleged killers: John Doyle Lee.

Throughout his Arizona years, Lee had formed a habit of sneaking back to pay conjugal visits to his other wives. He probably was unaware that he was the subject of an intensive manhunt when he called on his wife in Panquitch during the fall. When federal officers pounded on the front door of the house, Lee ran out the back door and hid in the outhouse. Then, realizing he could not escape, he sheepishly stumbled out and surrendered.

John Lee's first trial for murder ended with a hung jury. Eight Mormon jurors voted for acquittal and the four Gentiles held out for conviction. Lee was not so lucky the second time. In September 1876, he was found guilty and sentenced to death by firing squad.

On the chilly morning of March 23, 1876, Lee was taken back to Mountain Meadows for his execution. He sat calmly on the edge of his coffin while a photographer readied a camera to record the scene. If Lee felt any remorse for his crimes, he did not show it. Rather, he simply seemed quite resentful about being the only one ever punished for the massacre. "I am being sacrificed to spare others!" he shouted as he rose to stand at the foot of his coffin.

A blindfold was placed over his eyes; the firing squad raised its rifles and Mountain Meadows echoed once again with the sound of gunfire.

Within a year of John Lee's death, Emma remarried. She and her new husband, Franklin French, moved from Lee's Ferry to Winslow, taking the sack of gold nuggets John Lee had tucked under Emma's bed. Reportedly, they sold the gold for $7,000. John Lee, without having known he had done so, had given the newlyweds a lavish wedding present.

Meanwhile Robert Hilderbrand, now an adult, stayed on at Lee's Ferry, constantly thinking of the seven buckets of gold. He knew that each of these pails, if they actually existed, surely contained at least as much treasure as that single sack beneath the bed.

Where were these buckets? Time and again, Hilderbrand tried to retrace his step-father's footsteps. He explored Soap Creek Canyon and its environs many times but found nothing.

Lee's successor at the ferry, Warren Johnson, was another early searcher. He talked frequently to the older prospectors who came and went across the Colorado. A number of them remembered John Lee well; they said they had sometimes run across him far downstream, 60 to 70 miles below the ferry in the country known as Little Colorado. Johnson attempted to follow these old-timers' directions, but the area was so vast and rugged he always came back empty handed.

Rumors of a treasure map allegedly given by John to Emma Lee began circulating around 1880. Issac Haight, who was the bishop of Iron County, Utah, and also a participant in the Mountain Meadows Massacre, showed up on Emma French's doorstep in 1882 to demand that the map be turned over to him. His arrogance so offended Emma that she refused to talk to him.

One year later, Haight sent two more polite men, Sam and Bill Bass, to discuss the map with Emma. The Bass brothers must have been much more diplomatic, since Emma French agreed to tell them all she knew.

"There is no map," she told them. "Had there been one, Franklin and I would have put it to good use long before now. Nonetheless, I do firmly believe that John's gold must be hidden somewhere in or near Soap Creek Canyon. It is true that he traveled far and wide during his early prospecting trips, but toward the last, John was seldom gone for more than three or four days at a time. The gold and the mine it came from cannot be far from Lee's Ferry."

Emma French went on to say she did not believe the mine was an actual shaft or an excavation since John Lee never carried the kind of equipment needed for extensive mining. Instead she thought it likely her late husband had discovered a ledge or rock outcropping from which he could chip out the nuggets fairly easily.

Bill and Sam Bass hurried off to Soap Creek Canyon. Although their hopes were high, their luck was bad; they, like Robert Hilderbrand, found not a trace of gold. Nor did any of the scores of other prospectors who searched the area during the next 25 years. Then, at long last, the search came to a curious end. John Lee's gold was finally discovered in a nearly unbelievable way, but the discovery only led to the creation of a new mystery.

The final episode in the story began one night in 1909, while a young cowboy named Rowland Rider kept watch over a small herd of cattle not far from Soap Creek Canyon. He had just poured himself an after-supper cup of coffee when an odd-looking old man leading a mule stepped out of the darkness and into the circle of light surrounding Rider's campfire.

"Hope I ain't intrudin'," he ventured cautiously. "I seen your fire and thought I'd come by and say howdy."

Rider eyed his ragged visitor closely. He seemed harmless enough, he had a friendly smile and a blissfully bewildered expression on his face. "Howdy to you, too, stranger," Rider finally responded. "But what might you be doin' out here in the middle of nowhere?"

"Prospectin'," the old timer asserted. "I'm headin'

for Soap Creek Canyon to find John Lee's gold."

Rowland Rider couldn't help but chuckle as he handed the old man a cup of coffee. "Mister, you're headin' the wrong way. Soap Creek's back behind you. Tomorrow, I'll point you in the right direction."

At daybreak, Rider took him to the top of a rocky knoll from which he showed him the lay of the land and sent him on his way. Shortly after sundown, the old codger stumbled once again into the cowboy's lonely camp. "Dang me!" the old man muttered. "I must've gone round in a complete circle. I'm right back where I started from, ain't I? Well, I'll give it another go in the mornin.'"

When dawn came, the aged wanderer tottered off into the desolate landscape, only to return to Rowland Rider's campfire shortly before moonrise. This time, however, he was walking with a spritely step and laughing merrily. "I found it!" he shouted happily.

"The canyon?" Rider asked.

"No!" the old man declared. "John Lee's gold! I come across seven rusted-out old tin buckets chuck full of nuggets. Got it all packed up on my mule. Take a look at this, my friend." He untied one of his saddle bags, tugged out a canvas sack and tossed it to the perplexed cowboy. Rowland Rider opened the sack and promptly sat down on the ground in speechless amazement; the simple canvas pouch was completely filled with rough-edged golden nuggets.

"Help yourself to a fistful," the old timer urged. "I got six more bags just like that one. Say, you wouldn't happen to have any leftover beans you could warm up for me, would you? I'm powerful hungry."

A very dazed cowboy set his skillet back on the fire and asked, "So, what're you gonna do now, old man?"

"Reckon I'll head for Jacob's Pools and open

myself a bank account," the newly rich prospector replied. "Then I'll get properly outfitted and provisioned and go back to find the mine them nuggets come from. It can't be too far from where I found the buckets."

He stared into the campfire for a few moments before he said, "You know, I'll probably need me a partner, somebody to keep me from strayin' too far off course. I don't suppose you'd be interested in teamin' up with me, would you?"

Rider stirred the beans thoughtfully. "I got to look after this herd for another week," he said. "After my relief gets here, I'm free to go anywhere I want. Why don't I meet you in Jacob's Pools ten days from now?"

"Looks like we got ourselves a deal," the old man grinned as he shook Rider's hand. Next morning, the old fellow waved goodbye and led his mule toward the rut road that followed the Vermillion Cliffs to the fledgling town of Jacob's Pools. Ten days later, Rowland Rider rode off in the same direction.

Once Rider arrived in town, he went directly to the local assayer's office and inquired about the prospector. No one there had seen him. Next, he went to the bank, then to the saloons, and finally to the sheriff's office. By evening it was clear the old man had never made it to Jacob's Pools.

Young Rowland galloped off in search of the old duffer, but after combing the countryside for days, he found not a single sign of his would-be partner's passage. What became of this hapless wayfarer? Did he get lost again and perish in the wasteland? Or was he bushwhacked, robbed and murdered? His fate, like his name, is one of the desert's unrevealed secrets. And John Lee's mine, the fabled Golden Ledge —that, too, still belongs to the desert.

Where to Search for the Golden Ledge

Soap Creek can be approached either from Flagstaff or Fredonia. From Flagstaff, drive north on Alternative 89 for 14 miles to Navajo Bridge to cross the Colorado River. Eight miles further on Alternate 89, Soap Creek carves its way down to the river and enters Marble Canyon at Soap Creek Rapids. Its south fork wanders in from the southwest just below the highway. If you drive down from Fredonia, take Alternate 89 east to Jacob Lake and follow along the grand escarpment of the Vermillion Cliffs to the Soap Creek area. Topographic maps for Marble Canyon, Arizona, detail this wild landscape quite precisely. Don't expect to come out with your pockets stuffed with gold nuggets, but plan to enjoy some fine hiking.

Bibliography - Chapter 9

Corle, Edwin. **Listen, Bright Angel.** New York. Duell, Sloan and Pearce. 1946.

Mitchell, John D. **Lost Mines and Buried Treasurers of the Great Southwest.** Glorieta, New Mexico. Rio Grande Press. 1970.

O'Dea, Thomas F. **The Mormons.** Chicago. The University of Chicago Press. 1957.

Sasser, Charles W. *Old West* magazine. Stillwater, Oklahoma. Western Publications. Fall, 1957.

Thompson, George. *Desert* magazine. Palm Desert, California. July, 1980.

Wise, William. **Massacre at Mountain Meadows.** New York. Thomas Y. Crowell Company. 1976.

10
Secret of the Bisbee Maze

Arizona has certainly seen more than its share of authentic western heroes. Surely no other state in the Southwest can boast as many men who became legends by strapping on pistols and walking, like Gary Cooper, down dusty streets at high noon. From the OK Corral to the Whiskey Rows of the rip-roaring mining camps, Arizona's early lawmen blazed their way into the history books, becoming the most dramatic symbols of the Old West.

It is true, of course, that many of these bold and deadly men were less than honorable. Still, most were highly principled and possessed a near-suicidal commitment to the enforcement of the laws of the territory and to the oaths of office they swore to uphold. One of the most gallant and stoic of these fearless peace officers was a quiet, soft-spoken man named Harry C. Wheeler. To say that Harry Wheeler was esteemed and admired by almost everyone who met him would be an understatement. Anyone who had ever helped him chase an outlaw, or stood beside him in a gunfight, respected him almost to the point of hero-worship. Wheeler believed in enforcing the letter of the law and in defending the rights of every citizen within his jurisdiction. He never compromised on his principles.

Then one sultry summer morning in 1917, after 15 years of unblemished service as an exemplary lawman, Harry Wheeler broke the law for the first time in his life. He did not just bend the law; he broke it so spectacularly that President Woodrow Wilson ordered a special commission to investigate the incident.

To many of Wheeler's friends and admirers, his illegal action seemed so totally out of character that they wondered if he had suddenly abandoned his principles or gone crazy. An equal number of citizens approved of what he had done, but even they were uncertain as to his true motivation. Only Harry Wheeler himself knew why he committed the crime with which he was later charged. For reasons all his own, he chose not to talk about it for a long time.

To understand what kind of man Harry Wheeler was, one must look back at the early years of his life. He was born in Florida in 1876, the only son of Colonel William B. Wheeler, a career officer in the United States Army. Harry's grandfather had commanded a regiment during the Civil War, and it was taken for granted that young Harry would continue his family's proud military tradition by becoming a distinguished officer himself.

However, when he applied for admission into the United States Military Academy at West Point, he was rejected because he stood one-half inch short of the minimum height requirement. Through no fault of his

SHERIFF HARRY C. WHEELER. Did the famous lawman turn bad?

own, Harry Wheeler disappointed his father in the worst possible way. Perhaps it was his father's scorn that caused him to leave home and head west in 1900. Some historic accounts say he worked as a common laborer in Oklahoma before drifting on to southern Arizona where he found employment in the Cochise County copper mines.

In 1903, Wheeler enlisted as a private in the newly-formed Arizona Rangers. Within three months, he was promoted to sergeant. The Rangers, a small, elite territorial police force, had been created two years earlier to combat Arizona's ever-expanding wave of criminal activity. At the time, cattle rustlers near the Mexican border had grown so numerous that many ranchers were being forced out of business. Train robberies were common occurrences; the mountain wildernesses were infested with "robbers' roosts" where whole gangs of outlaws took refuge between robberies. The situation had gotten so far out of hand that it was impossible for the local lawmen to handle it by themselves. A special force of exceptional peace officers was created by the territorial legislature.

Captain Burton C. Mossman, the first head of the Arizona Rangers, selected his men with extreme care, choosing only those who were "good riders and shooters in top physical condition." Mossman's Rangers wasted no time in making a name for themselves. They cleaned out the outlaws' camps in the Blue Mountains and captured the ruthless mass murderer Augustine Chacon. With the help of the Mexican *Rurales*, they rid the border of bandits and smugglers.

The life of an Arizona Ranger was one of constant danger. The long manhunts always entailed great risks, but violence could also come suddenly and unexpectedly, as Wheeler found out one hot afternoon in Tucson.

He was walking along Congress Street when a terrified young man burst through the swinging doors of the Palace Saloon and ran into the street.

"Ranger!" the man shouted, "There's a holdup goin' on in there! An outlaw's got everybody lined up against the wall!" Instantly Wheeler drew his pistol and plunged through the still-swinging saloon doors. The outlaw spun around and both men fired simultaneously at nearly point blank range. The outlaw missed; Wheeler did not.

According to eye-witnesses, the Ranger knelt beside the dying gunslinger and said, "I'm sorry I had to kill you." The outlaw allegedly replied, "No hard feelin's on my part."

Shortly thereafter, Harry Wheeler was commissioned a lieutenant. When Captain Thomas Rynning resigned in 1907, Wheeler was promoted to captain. He commanded the Arizona Rangers until 1909 when the famous unit was abolished by the budget-cutting twenty-first Territorial Legislative Assembly. The Rangers had been so successful during their brief seven-year existence that the legislators felt there was no longer a need for them. The Rangers had made over 1,800 arrests, tamed Arizona's wildest towns and had literally worked themselves out of a job.

In September 1909, Wheeler was appointed deputy United States marshall for the Tucson district, but later resigned to become a line rider in the Customs Service along the Mexican border. In 1912, during the year Arizona attained statehood, he ran for sheriff in Cochise County. With his widespread name recognition, he won the election by a sizeable margin.

By then, Arizona was starting to get down right civilized. Its rowdiest days were over, and the winds of respectability were blowing across the once-wild frontier. The roulette wheels had stopped spinning in 1907 when gambling was outlawed by the territorial legislature. The swinging doors of the saloons slapped shut in 1914 after the citizens voted to make their arid state a totally dry one.

New and sometimes exotic industries were introduced. Several innovative ranchers discovered that a peculiar two-legged critter imported from Africa was more profitable to raise than domestic cattle or sheep. More than a dozen ostrich ranches sprang up in the Phoenix area. Scores of cowboys gave up herding cattle to become "ostrichboys." Equipped with long shepherd's staffs, the ostrichboys tended the huge flocks of 300-pound, eight-foot-tall, flightless birds. Roundup time was pretty exciting as the boys rode their horses at breakneck speed alongside the troops of incredibly swift birds, hooked them, bent them to the ground and clipped off the gorgeous plummage that would soon adorn the ornate hats of the nation's most fashionable women.

Some Arizonans were finding occasional employment in the fledgling motion picture industry. The state was gaining recognition as the perfect location for making western movies. A small tourist industry was also emerging as the railroads brought trainloads of easterners eager to peer over the rim of the Grand Canyon. With the introduction of refrigerated freight cars, Arizona's vegetable and citrus fruit production expanded dramatically. Cotton was becoming a major export. Even so, it was copper mining that was the bedrock of the state's economy.

Prior to the turn of the century, copper mining had not been a very profitable industry in Arizona due to transportation difficulties and primitive mining techniques. But with the advent of railroads and pneumatic drills, the industry took off. During Harry Wheeler's first year as sheriff, the Warren Mining District in Cochise County produced 130 million pounds of raw, red metal.

"The Queen of the Copper Camps" was always Bisbee, which had boomed from a tiny mining camp to a thriving town with a population of more than 9,000. Five thousand of these residents were miners whose small but steady paychecks supported the flourishing local businesses. The miners were a stalwart bunch, hardworking and honest. Therefore it is quite ironic that Harry Wheeler, a former miner himself, committed the most controversial act of his life in a confrontation with these men.

The hardrock miners of Bisbee —the muckers, trammers, hoistmen and the nomadic "bindle stiffs" who wandered from camp to camp— had always been an extraordinary class of laborers. The tales told about the earliest of them rival the fictitious yarns about John Henry, the steel drivin' man. To the hardrock drilling miner, his work was not just a job; it was a profession.

The drillers worked in pairs, deep beneath the sun-scorched earth. In the dim light of strearite candles glowing in cast-iron sconces, one man held and turned the drill while the other struck it with a nine-pound hammer in a swift, rhythmic cycle of mighty blows. Obviously, this feat required perfect coordination, for just one miss could mean a crushed hand for the man turning the drill. Many hardrock drillers were able to work at incredible speeds. Every Fourth of July, they proudly displayed their skills for the townspeople of Bisbee. A rock drilling contest was held each year following a festive parade. Giant granite boulders were hauled into town and dumped from the beds of wagons in the center of Main Street. Then, one after another, a succession of powerful, superbly muscled men stepped forward, spit on their hands and picked up their hammers. Each man's partner carefully positioned the drill, and the driller began to swing.

The object was to see which man could bore the deepest hole in solid granite during a given length of time. Almost any miner who entered the contest was capable of striking the drill at least 60 times within 60 seconds, but there were a legendary few who worked so fast that no observer could count their strokes. The fastest of them all was a giant of a man named Fred Yorkey. Some of the old timers claimed Yorkey's hammer rang 140 times a minute, but no one could be sure because all anyone ever saw was a blur. Yorkey worked so fast that his coach had to steadily pour water into the hole to keep the drill from burning up. In 1907, he set what was believed to be a world record: 28 and five-eighths inches in three minutes.

Only one other man ever came close to seriously challenging Yorkey's championship, and he did so despite a severe handicap. This driller, O.M. King, had been blinded in a mining accident, but he continued to work and was said to be a faster driller than most men with keen vision. King often placed second in the contests. Hardrock drilling by hammer became a lost art in 1910 when pneumatic jackhammers were introduced in the copper mines. But the new mining techniques in no way diminished the miners' pride in their work. In fact, their higher production gave them the additional satisfaction of knowing that their labor was the primary reason that Bisbee had become such a fine town.

Each day when the weary miners came up from the tunnels after their long hours of toil, they walked along Main Street and Brewery Gulch Avenue, past the Copper Queen Hotel, the Orpheum theatre, the elegant Edelweiss restaurant and the new public library. They glanced up at the fancy mansions perched on the hillsides where the copper bosses and the bankers lived. Then they trudged on to their own humble dwellings. Though they had a lot of civic pride, the miners could not help but resent the fact that they who did the hardest work profited the least.

For the new sheriff, Bisbee was a pretty tame town compared to the other places he worked in his earlier years. Bisbee's infamous red light district, with its dance halls, cribs and opium dens, had been outlawed by the city council two years before Harry Wheeler took office, and criminal activity had gone into a rapid decline. From time to time, Wheeler raided a bootlegger's whiskey still or arrested an occasional thief, but overall, Bisbee was pretty tranquil... until April 6, 1917.

On that historic day, the Congress of the United States adopted a resolution declaring war on Germany. A great surge of patriotism swept the nation. On every Main Street in America, people from all classes of society paraded in unity beneath red, white and blue flags and banners alongside the youthful "doughboys" who were marching off to fight the bloodthirsty Huns. Arizona exceeded all other states in the per capita percentage of soldiers and sailors who were drafted or enlisted in the armed forces. And the state made an even greater contribution to the war effort through its production of that crucially important wartime metal, copper.

The copper mines of Bisbee went into high gear; soon they were shipping out an unprecedented 190 million pounds annually. The price of copper skyrocketed from eleven cents a pound to 37 and a half cents. Fortunes were being made overnight by the mining companies and their eastern investors.

The miners themselves, however, reaped no new benefits. They were still being paid the same three dollars and fifty cents a day, while watching wartime inflation further erode their limited buying power. Additionally, the speeded-up rate of production was making an already hazardous occupation more dangerous than ever.

Underground mining has always been an extremely perilous job: a 1911 report in the *Engineering and Mining Journal* showed the Bisbee Copper Queen to be one of the most injury-plagued operations in the nation. During that one year, eight miners were killed, 76 were seriously hurt, and 686 sustained minor injuries. Every miner who stepped daily into the hoisting cage to descend to the subterranean network of tunnels beneath Sacramento Hill knew he might never see the light of day again.

Death below ground was always sudden, unforeseen and inevitably gruesome. Falling rock slabs crushed many a man, and rotted water-impregnated ladders often collapsed, sending workers plunging hundreds of feet into the darkness. The fast-moving cages often became death traps. Poorly timed detonations of dynamite killed and maimed scores of miners. As an old miners' ballad put it: "Many a mother's son knelt down to pray" before entering the depths of the Copper Queen.

By June 1917, most of the miners had decided they could no longer tolerate the unfair wages and unsafe conditions. They sent representatives of the International Union of Mine, Mill and Smelter Workers to the offices of the Calumet & Arizona, Shattuck &

Arizona, and Phelps Dodge corporations with a list of demands. Wages, they said, would have to be raised to six dollars a day, and the sliding pay scale which paid Mexican and other foreigners less than U.S. citizens would have to be eliminated. They pointed out that when copper prices fell, wages were lowered accordingly, but when the prices rose, the wages stayed the same. Secondly, the union said, safety conditions absolutely had to be improved. There would have to be better timbering, buttressing and ventilation, more care in the use of explosives and transport cages. They called for regular safety inspections and a lot of additional latrine carts.

The corporate officials countered by reminding them that the Bisbee miners were already being paid more than their fellow workers in Jerome and Lowell. If they wanted extra money, they had the option of working on Sundays. As far as safety was concerned, the miners were chided for being unwilling to take a few risks on the home front while their own sons and brothers faced death every day on the battlefields of France. The union's demands were unreasonable, the managers said; there was nothing more to be discussed.

The union negotiators left the company's plush offices with grim expressions on their faces. That night, they called a meeting of the rank and file membership. A vote was taken; in the morning the second largest copper mine in the United States was shut down by a strike. The entire surface crew and nearly half of the underground workers walked off the job to form picket lines at the mine entrances, the railroad depot and the ore-loading docks.

Management reacted with predictable outrage. "Strikes are inimical in peacetime and treasonable in time of war," thundered Phelps Dodge President Walter Douglas. "There will be no compromise, because you cannot compromise with rattlesnakes!"

"We will not yield to extortion," stated John Greenway, general manager of Calumet & Arizona.

The miners themselves were far from united on the decision to strike. Many felt the walk-out was, indeed, unpatriotic and wished to continue working. Bisbee's business community expressed its opposition to the strike, and most stores cut off credit to any miner refusing to work. As news of the strike spread, "outside agitators" began arriving in droves. The Industrial Workers of the World (IWW) sent in teams of organizers to exhort the strikers to greater militancy. The Wobblies, as they were called, urged the already defiant miners to use whatever means necessary to keep the mines closed down. They openly advocated "direct action and sabotage" as a way to do that.

In response, Bisbee merchants banded together in a Citizens' Protective League to guard their properties against vandalism, while at least a thousand miners who were still loyal to the mining companies formed an anti-union Workman's Loyalty League. Phelps Dodge hastily brought in several "goon squads" composed of hard-eyed, brutal professional strikebreakers ready at the slightest excuse to wade into the picket line with truncheons and brass knuckles. In just two weeks' time, peaceful little Bisbee became a powderkeg with a smoldering fuse.

Sheriff Wheeler did what he could, but society was breaking down; the town grew more violent and lawless each day. He knew the fuse was burning shorter. If he could not contain the most volatile situation he had ever encountered, the whole town was going to blow wide open. As a former miner, he knew the strikers' grievances were legitimate; he sympathized with them. But as a patriot from a long line of military officers, he worried about the mine closure's impact on the war effort in Europe. Caught between corporations that refused to negotiate and the strikers' willingness to endure any hardship or danger to win their struggle, Wheeler sided with neither faction. His duty, as he saw it, was to keep the peace.

He gave careful instructions to his deputies: "I want to impress upon each of you the absolute necessity for extreme self-control, cool, calm judgement and patience. Avoid all display of weapons. Remember, you are deputized for the maintenance of peace."

Behind the scenes, the top echelon of the mine management and the Citizens' Protective League held nightly strategy meetings. On the evening of July 11, they asked Sheriff Wheeler to join them in John Greenway's office. After everyone shook hands all around, Greenway said, "Harry, we've come up with a plan to break the strike —to end it very quickly and very forcefully." He handed Wheeler a sheet of paper. "We've drawn up a deportation order for you to sign. We want you to round up all the strikers and ship them clear out of the state."

Harry Wheeler stared at the paper in disbelief. "This is an illegal order," he said. "Those men out there have committed no crimes. I can't arrest people for exercising their right to strike."

"You can arrest them for any reason you want, Harry. Vagrancy. Disorderly conduct. Disturbing the peace. Or even treason. Just remember, we're behind you all the way." Greenway reached out his hand to pat the sheriff on the shoulder, but Wheeler stepped away. His dark eyes narrowed. The grim expression on his face was that of a man who had been deeply

offended. He tossed the deportation order back on
Greenway's desk, turned away in disgust and slammed
the door on his way out of the room.

Wheeler strode back down the darkened streets
to his own office. He was just reaching for the door
knob when a figure stepped out of the shadows and
furtively beckoned to him. Wheeler paused momentarily, then walked over to the man. The sheriff listened to
what the man said, nodded his head, and went with
him into the darkness.

It was after midnight when Harry Wheeler
returned to his office. He immediately sat down at his
desk, lifted the receiver of his telephone, and got John
Greenway out of bed. "I've changed my mind," the
sheriff said. "I'll carry out your plan." He then began
calling his deputies and, when they were all assembled
before him, he explained, "We're going to arrest every
striker in town, put them all on a train, and ship them
out of Arizona."

The deputies exchanged glances. They knew their
boss was a stern man, but never before had they heard
the hard, cold tone of voice he now used. One of the
deputies cleared his throat and said, "Sheriff... begging
your pardon, sir... but this doesn't sound like a legal
action. We're going to catch all kinds of hell if we do
this."

"I'm taking full responsibility," Wheeler replied.
"Obey my orders or turn in your badge. Muster every
member of the Citizens' Protective League and tell
them I want them fully armed." He drew his watch
from his vest pocket. "The roundup starts at six a.m.
Get moving."

The first rays of dawn were just beginning to
push back the shadows in the canyon town of Bisbee
when the hastily-organized teams of rifle-toting vigi-

lantes spread out along the streets below the miners' housing. At six on the dot, Sheriff Wheeler gave the command that sent the enormous posse swarming into the strikers' homes. Doors were kicked open, dazed miners were pulled from their beds, breakfast tables were overturned and, as wives and children screamed, hundreds of half-dressed men were shoved at gunpoint into the white glare of a desert morning.

When the vigilantes stormed the boarding house where Wobblie organizer James Brew was staying, Brew greeted the intruders with a burst of gunfire that killed one of the Leaguers. He was quickly and effectively overcome by a deadly barrage from a dozen rifles. Anyone who resisted or protested was clubbed to the ground and pistol-whipped. Within less than an hour, more than a thousand stunned strikers had been herded into the broad intersection in front of the flag-bedecked post office. Sheriff Wheeler stood on the edge of the crowd, but when the miners saw him they began to jeer and shout.

"You bastard, Harry!" cried a man with a bloody face. "Sold out to the copper bosses, didn't ya? How much did they pay ya, Harry?"

Harry Wheeler's eyes were hidden in the shadow of his wide-brimmed hat, but his mouth was a tight, straight line across his firm jaw. "March them all over to the ball park," he instructed his deputies. "Then go back and arrest that Wobbly lawyer, Bill Cleary, along with any merchant or businessman who in any way supported the strike. I want every last one of them on board the train that's going to pull out of here at noon."

By mid-morning, 1,186 men stood in the wilting heat of the fenced-in ball park. At eleven o'clock, a 23-car freight train chuffed into town. As the miners' families gathered to watch, the miners were herded single file into cattle cars. An hour later, they were on their way to Columbus, New Mexico, where the deportees were placed temporarily in the stockades normally used to confine illegal immigrants from Mexico.

Back in Bisbee, Sheriff Wheeler virtually sealed the town. His deputies guarded every road and searched and interrogated everyone coming or going. Kangaroo courts were convened to interrogate the remaining miners about their loyalty to the copper companies and to their country. Anyone who gave answers considered less than satisfactory was ordered to leave town.

When word of the Bisbee deportations spread across the country, labor leaders and civil libertarians raised such a clamor that President Wilson empaneled a Mediation Commission headed by the Secretary of Labor to investigate the affair. The commission ruled that the deportations clearly violated the constitutional rights of the deportees, interfered with interstate commerce, and violated Arizona statutes relative to kidnapping. Charges were brought against Harry Wheeler, the principal mine managers and several public officials.

The trial was held in Tombstone and lasted only one day. The defense argued that the evacuation was justified as a communal act of self-defense in the face of a strike that jeopardized the safety of the public. The jury agreed; after 16 minutes of deliberation, they brought in a "not guilty" verdict. It was all over so quickly that Harry Wheeler was not even called to the stand to testify about his reasons for carrying out the copper bosses' illegal order.

But why *did* Wheeler suddenly reverse himself and take such drastic action? Much has been written about the Bisbee incident, but only one author addressed this particular question. Dane Coolidge, who was both an historian and a novelist during the 1920s and 30s, wrote that on the night of July 11, Wheeler was "taken down into the old workings of a mine." By whom, Coolidge did not say, but it was probably one of the old hardrock drillers, someone familiar with the original mines and their network of played-out, long-abandoned tunnels. Neither did Coolidge mention which mine the sheriff visited that night, but mostly likely it was the old Czar.

The Czar Mine was Bisbee's first successful copper producer. Opened in 1884 at a depth of only 400 feet, it became a maze of tunnels and shafts above which the railroad and the Copper Queen's smelters were eventually built. The man who guided Wheeler into this dark labyrinth undoubtedly cautioned him to watch his step as they descended the old, dry-rotted ladders nailed to the framing timbers in the shaft. When they reached the floor of the mine, he led Wheeler forward behind the bobbing circle of light cast by his lantern.

The old timer knew exactly where he was going and, as the two of them moved along, he did a little explaining: "You know, Harry, when a man walks a picket line all day like I been doin' these past few weeks, he hears a lotta talk. Just scuttlebutt mostly, but the other day I heard somethin' that scared the hell outta me... a rumor about somethin' that's down here in this mine. Had me so worried, I couldn't sleep. So I decided to come down here and take a look-see. Duck your head, Harry. There's a loose eyebeam right above your hat."

The two men had entered the Czar's oldest, dankest tunnels, the original drifts that had been drilled and blasted through the hard, grey limestone

more than 30 years before. Both men sweated profuse-
ly. It was hard to breathe. On either side of them, the
once-sturdy shoring timbers bulged under the enormous weight of the earth pressing down from above. In
places, the drifts cut through strata composed of loose
dirt held back by buttressed boards which were beginning to crack and shift. A score of startled rats scam-
pered away from the advancing light.

The old miner chuckled. "It's always good to see
rats. They're smart little varmints. If there's gonna be a
cave-in, they can feel it comin'. They're always the first
ones outta the mine. Well, we haven't got much farther
to go now. What I want to show you is just around this
next turn. Stay close behind me." He took a few more
careful steps, stopped and raised his lantern high.
"There it is, Harry. Take a look at that."

Sheriff Wheeler blinked in amazement. From
where he stood to the furthest reaches of the wavering
beam of light, the tunnel was crammed from floor to
ceiling with explosives, bundle after bundle of dynamite tied together with a latticework of detonating
wires. "I wouldn't go no closer if I was you," the miner
advised. "It's bound to be booby-trapped."

"Who did this?" the sheriff asked.

"Traitors," the old man replied. "German sympa-
thizers. I reckon they figure if the mine don't stay closed
down by the strike, they're gonna shut'er down permanent. They moved all the dynamite from the Copper
Queen's magazines into this one tunnel. There's sup-
posed to be a set of wires running' up a shaft back there
somewhere, and the ends are hidden up on the surface.
All they gotta do is hook'em up, push the plunger, and
this whole hillside, along with the railroad tracks, the
smelters and everything will blow sky-high and come
back down smack-dab in the middle of Main Street."

He paused a moment to let that image sink in. "Remember what happened in Lowell ten years ago? Four tons of dynamite stored in the Denn Mine magazine went off. Killed five drillers, and blew a 60-foot hole in the ground, and wrecked every building on the property. It busted every window in Lowell. That was a bad one... worst I ever seen... but, boy-howdy, if this one goes off, you can just say 'Goodbye, Bisbee.' These guys mean business."

"Who are they?" Wheeler asked.

"Wish I knew, Harry. Like I said, all I heard was rumors. Wobblies, maybe. Or some of them foreign boys. Or maybe, just somebody who hates this mine more'n he loves his country."

Wheeler exhaled a long-held breath. "Show me the way back out of here," he said curtly. "And make it fast." The old miner could scarcely keep up with the sheriff as they tramped through the dark corridors and reclimbed the rickety ladders. After they reached the fresh, night air, the old man asked a favor: "You won't tell nobody it was me that tipped you off, will you, Harry? If those guys knew I was the one, they'd kill me for sure."

"Don't worry," Wheeler assured him. "Go on home now. And... thanks." The sheriff quickly crossed the railroad tracks, went back to his office and placed his call to John Greenway. During the tumultuous morning that followed, Wheeler kept silent about the dynamite, undoubtedly because he feared any mention of it would start a panic or prompt the perpetrators to set off the massive charge from an unknown location. In all probability, he shipped his special confidant out of town along with the others in order to protect the old man's identity.

For several days after the evacuation, Wheeler

searched high and low for the surface ends of the wire. According to Coolidge, they were never found. And what became of the dynamite itself? Coolidge doesn't say, nor does any other historian. Was it carefully defused and removed from the dark depths of the Czar? Or was it simply sealed off until it decayed and became harmless? The only certainty is that Wheeler told very few people about the explosives until he was sure they no longer posed a threat.

When he finally did speak up, a number of people called him a liar. They swore he invented the whole story to cover up his real motivation, which, they believed, was a big, fat bribe from the copper companies. However, there are   several good reasons to accept Harry Wheeler's version of what took place that night, July 11, 1917. All of the historical accounts acknowledge that rumors of a hidden cache of dynamite were definitely circulating among the strikers. Although no verification of the rumors was presented during the brief trial, the defense was able to argue successfully that there was a widespread fear in Bisbee of "a sinister plot hatched by foreigners, anarchists or Bolsheviks against the American way of life."

Then, the moral character of Harry Wheeler must be taken into consideration. Prior to his Bisbee deportations, he had a reputation for total honesty. He was hardly the sort of man who would suddenly sell his honor by accepting a bribe. But when he ran for re-election, he was defeated. Too many voters no longer trusted him. After that, he went from job to job until he died a poor man in 1925.

Harry Wheeler broke the law only once in his life. Was his brutal action against the striking miners justified as a means of saving the town he had sworn to protect? Would Bisbee have been blown to bits without his prompt and outrageous actions? Perhaps the answer lies in a long-forgotten caved-in tunnel. Maybe the rats are the only ones who know for sure.

How to Visit the Tunnel Mazes of Bisbee

Rail tours through the old Copper Queen Mine are conducted four times a day, year around. The tours, which last approximately 75 minutes, leave from the Queen Mine Tour Building located directly south of Old Bisbee's business district, off the U.S. Highway 80 interchange. These old tunnels have been re-timbered, and there is adequate natural ventilation. But many more miles of abandoned mining drifts remain closed.

During the tour of the Copper Queen underground, ex-miners explain how turn-of-the-century mines were operated. Passengers are all furnished with a slicker, a hard hat and a battery-pack light, but it is wise to also wear a sweater or jacket since it is usually chilly deep below ground.

Bibliography - Chapter 10

Bailey, Lynn R. **Bisbee, Queen of the Copper Camps.** Tucson. Westernlore Press. 1983.

Burgess, Opie Rundle. **Bisbee, Not So Long Ago.** San Antonio, Texas. The Naylor Company. 1967.

Coolidge, Dane. **Fighting Men of the West.** New York. E.P. Hutton. 1932.

Miller, Joseph. **The Arizona Rangers.** New York. Hastings House. 1972.

Wagoner, Jay. **Arizona's Heritage.** Salt Lake City. Peregrine Smith Books. 1983.

11

"I Shall Kill Them All But One!"

It was 1926, a year of hip flasks and Hupmobiles. Prohibition was in effect, and gang leaders were shooting each other in Chicago. Charles Lindberg was building the Spirit of St. Louis, and the Cardinals had won the World Series. In this dazzling era of bootleggers, jazz-bos and flappers, the Old West was just a distant, romantic memory; cowboys and Indians now fought only in flickering images on the silent screen.

But in some of the more remote parts of the country, in places like southern Arizona and below the border in Sonora, life was still being lived in the old ways, by the old rules. For a good many of the people who inhabited these isolated areas, the Twentieth Century had not yet arrived. Their world was just as hard and simple as it had been for their pioneering grandparents. And at times it was just as perilous.

In October 1926, a wealthy Mexican cattleman, Francisco Fimbres, was returning home with his family after a business trip to the small Sonoran town of Naco. Although the trail wound its way through heavy mesquite, Fimbres, his wife, young daughter and infant son rode nonchalantly, expecting no trouble. Suddenly gunfire erupted from the brush. Señora Fimbres fell from her horse, mortally wounded. Francisco grabbed the reins of his daughter's rearing mount and galloped for the nearest arroyo.

The dying woman, still clutching her baby, tried to crawl for cover, but the Apache ambushers were upon her in a moment. They tore her baby from her arms and ran. Fimbres left his daughter in the comparative safety of the ravine, scrambled up the bank and dashed back to the ambush site. One glance told him it was too late.

He dropped to his knees and lifted his wife from the blood-soaked sand. Later, he would report that her last words had been: "They took our son. Swear to get him back." Then she drooped lifeless in his arms. Francisco Fimbres rocked her back and forth in stunned grief. "I swear," he said as he wept, "I swear I will find him. And I will avenge you." This oath, sworn in the empty desolation of a hot Sonoran wasteland, would obsess Fimbres for nearly a decade, and it would stir the emotions of two nations.

In that year, 1926, almost all Apaches were settled on reservations. The long years of exile in Florida, Alabama and Oklahoma were behind them. They were back in their homelands, re-defining themselves and struggling to take their places in a new society. Apache children were attending school, learning to read and write, and to play basketball. Only the elders still remembered the nomadic freedom of the past.

But deep in the wilds of Sonora, small bands of outlaw Apaches still roamed. The Mexicans called them *Los Bronchos*, the untamed ones. From their strongholds deep in the trackless expanse of the Sierra Madre, they continued to make sporadic attacks on ranches in Mexico and Arizona, just as their ancestors had done.

Francisco Fimbres had faced this menace more than once. In 1913, Apaches had raided his ranch and stolen many horses and cattle. He and several neighbors had set out in hot pursuit. They overtook the *Bronchos* before they reached the mountains. In the skirmish that followed, several Indians were killed and a 14-year-old Apache girl was taken prisoner. Rather than turn her over to the Mexican authorities, Fimbres took her to his ranch, where he had her trained as one of his servants. Although she adapted well to ranch life and became almost like a member of the family, the Apache renegades never forgot that a man named Fimbres had stolen one of their women. Years passed, and finally when Francisco Fimbres had children of his own, the Apaches struck back. The way the Apaches saw it, an old debt was paid.

With his wife dead and his son's fate uncertain, the grief-stricken rancher desperately sought government aid to finance an expedition to hunt down the kidnappers. Although the Sonoran government longed to be rid of the marauding Apaches, it feared troop movements might provoke hostilities with the militant Yaqui Indians who inhabited the same area. Rather than trade one Indian problem for another, the Mexican officials refused the cattleman's request. Undaunted, Fimbres organized a posse of his own ranch hands and rode off for the Sierra Madre.

The Sierra Madre is the spine of Mexico. Its ragged outline splits the country from north to south like a 400-mile row of dorsal fins, forming a nearly impenetrable barrier between Sonora and Chihuahua. Beyond its dry, alluvial plains, the Sierra Madre crashes against the sky in fold after fold of blue peaks. The rugged slopes are slashed and gouged by deep brush-choked ravines amid an endless network of serrated ridges leading to high alpine plateaus.

For more than two years, Fimbres and his *vaqueros* rode those pathless ridges. He neglected his huge ranch and ate into his personal fortune to go back, time and again, to the mountains. It was like searching for ghosts; the Apaches always faded wraith-like ahead of him, leaving only faint tracks and abandoned campsites. Yet sometimes, in these empty camps, the rancher found the footprints of small children. So he pushed on; one of the children might be his son.

While his searches brought no results, his continued negotiations with the Mexican government finally paid off. On January 3, 1929, Fimbres received a commission from the Sonoran governor, Fausto Topeto, to organize a search party at the border town of Agua Prieta to hunt down and wipe out the Apache band. Adventurers from both sides of the border eagerly volunteered. Fimbres hand-picked his posse, choosing only men skilled in the deadly art of hunting other men. Many of the ones he selected had already gained impressive reputations as Indian killers.

There was Sam Hayhurst, an expert tracker who had chased Apaches in Arizona until 1922. Next was the aged ex-cavalryman, Anton Massonovitch, a veteran of the Geronimo campaign. Maroni Finn, who had prospected in the Sierra Madre, joined up along with more than 60 hunters and trappers. On January 5, a truck convoy rolled out of the border town carrying an advance party of eleven men. The group was heavily armed and equipped with provisions for two weeks.

The other 50 men waited at the border, ready to move out when word came that the Apaches had been found. The advance group left the trucks at Colonias Morales, where they mounted horses and rode east into the area called the Canyon of Caves.

Fimbres' expedition did not escape the attention of the press. Sensational stories about the "Last Indian Campaign" quickly appeared in Arizona newspapers. The reporters' imaginations were stimulated by the coincidental fact that Fimbres' ranch on the Bavispe River was nearly the spot where Geronimo surrendered in 1886. The newspapers announced that the Apache outlaws were the descendants of Geronimo's band.

That report brought quick denials from the Mescalero Reservation in New Mexico. Old Chief Chatto denied that any of Geronimo's people could have left descendants in Mexico. Chatto had served as a scout for the U.S. Army against Geronimo and still wore the enormous silver medal awarded him by President Grover Cleveland. Other former scouts, Nartine, Kayi-tah, and Jaspar Kansean, all in their seventies, verified Chatto's statement. Only one old man and one old woman had escaped, they said; everyone else surren-dered or was killed.

Most of the newspapers chose to ignore this information, since the concept of a Mexican rancher riding off to fight the sons of Geronimo was too dra-matic to resist. An unrelated incident inspired the journalists to become even more creative.

On January 7, just two days after Fimbres' advance party set out, a cowhand named Van Phillips finished his lunch at the Carreta Ranch south of

Hachita, New Mexico, and rode back to Millsite Creek
to retrieve a cow he had left there earlier. When he
didn't show up for supper, his saddle pals went looking
for him. They came back to report Phillips had vanished without a trace.

"Cowboy Kidnapped by Apaches; Taken to Sierras," the New Mexico newspapers proclaimed. The
Albuquerque Journal quoted the ranch foreman, A.L.
Boyd, as saying, "It is known Apaches have been in
this locality recently. A 40-man posse of cowboys and
county officials is being organized, and the Rural Police
of Chihuahua are also joining the search." Suddenly
there were two Last Indian Campaigns going at once,
and the press made sure the general public was kept
well-informed about the armed men galloping off into
"the lair of a wild band of Apaches." Within a week, the
Chihuahua *Rurales* found Van Phillips' body and definitely determined he had been killed by Mexican bandits. Nevertheless, the international boundary was now
being called "The Apache Frontier."

Back in the adjoining border towns of Agua Prieta and Douglas, Arizona, Fimbres' backup force was
growing apprehensive. No word had come back from
the advance party, making it almost certain they had
run into trouble. Then, in mid-January, one of the
eleven returned. Ramon Quejada was carried into Agua
Prieta by Sonoran peasants who had found him half-
dead in the foothills. Delirious, burning with fever,
Quejada raved about an ordeal of incredible hardship.

In the Canyon of the Caves, the terrain was too
steep for horses, so the group had struggled ahead on
foot. The temperatures were sub-zero and freezing
winds blasted them as they reached the higher eleva-
tions. Quejada grew too ill to continue; he had staggered back out of the canyon. The *alcalde* of Agua Pri-

eta immediately dispatched a rescue team led by Jesús Valdez, an expert tracker. Valdez backtracked Quejada until he caught up with Fimbres. Although he was nearing exhaustion, Fimbres refused to turn back. He had seen Apaches! The Indians had been flushed from their camp. Some of them were children.

Not until January 31, when their supplies completely ran out, did the advance party return. Having pushed themselves beyond the limits of their endurance, they decided to rest and wait for better weather.

For Francisco Fimbres, there could be no rest. By February 8, he was on his way back to the mountains. This time, only three men accompanied him: his life-long American friend, Frederick Humphries, Pedro Castro, godfather of the lost boy, and Maroni Finn, the prospector. Once again, forces beyond Fimbres' control decided the fate of his mission.

On March 4, the flames of revolution flared across Mexico. Insurgents seized towns and destroyed railroads near the border. Two American engineers were killed, and 2,000 U.S. infantrymen were mobilized, packed and ready to enter Mexico to protect American lives. Fimbres realized that if he did find the Apache stronghold, no reinforcements from Arizona would be allowed to enter the war-torn country to assist him. Again, he was forced to wait.

It was already turning winter again, in November 1929, before he could re-organize a full-scale campaign to hunt the Apache band. Word of his new punitive expedition flashed nationwide. In Arizona, Fimbres was regarded as something of a hero, but the eastern newspapers took a dimmer view. Many were appalled that this one man could appoint himself judge and executioner of an entire band of Indians.

Time magazine called him "Ferocious Fimbres." and denounced him in its December 9, 1929 issue: "The biggest news of the week in Mexico was a ferocious scheme calmly announced by the great landed proprietor, Francisco Fimbres, to put to death a whole tribe of Apache Indians, braves, squaws and papooses. Local papers praised 'Ferocious Fimbres.' He claimed to have every assurance that the Mexican government would not try to stop his private massacre.

"Mounted gunmen hired by 'Ferocious Fimbres' recently located the Apaches —a small tribe said to number only 25— on an almost inaccessible fortified plateau high in the Sierra Madre. 'This time they cannot escape,' Fimbres exulted last week. 'Blood of God's Mother, I have waited three years! It may take till spring but I shall kill them all but one —my own little boy, Heraldo.'"

Fimbres set up a recruiting office in Douglas where volunteers for his expedition could sign up. The response was overwhelming. Fimbres' recruiting officer, Douglas' chief of police, Leslie Gatliff, received more than 1,500 applications from all over the United States and Canada. Gatliff simply filed these letters away, since more men were showing up in person than he could possibly process. Every morning, scores of Arizona cowboys, professional mercenaries and amateur thrill-seekers were waiting on the sidewalk outside his office.

Everyone of these eager, would-be Indian fighters was sure the Old West was about to come roaring back to life again for the last time. None of them wanted to miss it. This was their last chance for glory, a chance to be able to tell their grandchildren: "I rode with Fimbres."

"Have you room for a fellow who has done two

hitches in the Marine Corps and one in the Navy?" an easterner named Ellsworth Drazy asked Gatliff. "I have fought in Haiti and Nicaragua and was in the landing at Vera Cruz. I guess I have the guts to chase these birds."

A Canadian volunteer, Jack Williams boasted, "I have traveled all over the globe and fought men of all colors. I would like to become one of your expedition, for I love action."

A Denver physician, R.G. Davenport, stepped up to the police chief's desk and hooked his thumbs in his vest pockets. "I shall count it a great privilege to join you," he said. "I have hunted big game in many parts of America, but I am sure shooting an Apache Indian would give me a greater thrill than anything I have heretofore shot."

Police Chief Gatliff's response to most of these wild-eyed characters was a polite "thank you" and a firm "goodbye." He knew that Fimbres needed men who were more than mere glory-hounds. The only ones he signed up were the ones who said: "Yes, I know what the Sierra Madre is like."

While Gatliff was selecting Fimbres' civilian army in Arizona, Colonel Hermangildo Carrillo moved 200 Mexican cavalrymen to Bacerac at the foot of the Sierra Madres. Telephone communications were opened between this outpost and Douglas. Arrangements were made for automobiles to shuttle men back and forth. The Mexican government promised to supply machine guns and airplanes. The final Indian campaign, climaxing two centuries of warfare, was ready to be launched against an estimated two dozen Apaches.

Then the Mexican government began to have second thoughts. The prospect of several hundred American adventurers swarming over the countryside was an alarming one. It was just the sort of thing that might lead to an incident that would provide an excuse for the U.S. Army to enter the politically unstable nation. The risk was too great. Mexico closed its borders to all volunteer Indian fighters. The Last Indian War ended before it began.

Francisco Fimbres' private war had only begun.

He returned to his Bavispe Valley ranch accompanied by a sizeable pack of hired gunmen. These men, along with most of Fimbres' cowhands, set up a network of continuous patrols throughout the area. When the Apaches stole a herd of cattle from a ranch in the Bacerac district in March 1930, Fimbres' gunfighters caught up with them and shot five from their horses before the rest scattered into the foothills.

Month after month, Fimbres relentlessly tracked the dwindling Apache band. Over a period of two years, the fanatical rancher personally killed three Indians while his brother, Cayetano, accounted for several more. Still, there was no sign of his son, for the surviving Apaches always managed to stay one step ahead of their pursuers. The years dragged by, but Fimbres never gave up hope. If his son was alive, he was sure that someday Heraldo would be found.

In November 1935, unusually heavy snows fell in the Sierra Madre. Although these mountains are hot and dry much of the year, winter snows can reach a depth of four feet, while blizzard winds may pile the snow into 30-foot drifts. The storm raging in the Sierras stirred new excitement in the bitter heart of Francisco Fimbres. He knew the storm was doing what he had never been able to do: drive the last Apaches down from the mountain stronghold.

Convinced the Indians would be coming to the lowlands, Fimbres set his trap. Nor far from the site of the original ambush, he drove a small herd of cattle into a box canyon. Then Francisco, Cayetano and the gunmen hid themselves nearby and settled back to wait.

If there was one thing Fimbres had learned in nine years of searching, it was patience. The strain of an endless hunt had left its mark on the Mexican cattleman. He was old before his time and hard of heart. But he knew how to wait. This time, his patience paid off. Before long, the outlaw Apaches entered the canyon.

The years had been hard on the *Bronchos*, too. There were only a dozen of them now, three of whom were women. Ragged, half-starved and desperate, they rode into a trap they would have avoided by instinct in the past. As they approached the herd, Fimbres' posse opened fire. Two of the male warriors fell, and the rest broke into confused flight. Francisco and Cayetano plunged through the snow, firing wildly at the fleeing figures.

This time no one escaped. When all the male Indians had been killed, the two brothers strode back to the mouth of the canyon where the Apache women had surrendered to the hired gunmen. They were standing with their eyes averted, their thin blankets drawn around their shoulders, waiting. Fimbres cocked his rifle and raised it to his shoulder.

"No!" Cayetano shouted. "Not the women, Francisco! Don't..." The roar of Fimbres' rifle drowned out his brother's voice. The women crumpled lifeless into the snow.

"You damned fool!" Cayetano gasped. "Do you realize what you've done? Everyone of them is dead. There is no one left to tell you where your son is!"

Fimbres' face grew pale. The empty rifle fell from

his hands. "Mother of God," he whispered as he turned his eyes toward the darkening mountains. Was Heraldo up there somewhere? Had the people he had just killed been raising and caring for his son just as he had raised and cared for the girl he stole from them so many years ago?

Fimbres had never given up hope that someday he would find his son. But now, if Heraldo was still alive, he was huddled with the other children, freezing, starving, waiting for the meat that would never come. Perhaps Heraldo had been dead for years. Yet some of the children's footprints Fimbres had seen so many times could have been those of his son. In those last moments of obsessive hatred, had he condemned his own son to a frozen death?

Bibliography - Chapter 11

Albuquerque Journal. January, 1929.

Associated Press. January, February, November, 1929, and January, April, 1930.

Bailey, L.R. **Indian Slave Trade in the Southwest.** Tower Publications. New York. 1966.

Time magazine. December 9, 1929.

12

Close Encounters
at Snowflake

Travis Walton glanced at his watch. It was six o'clock —quitting time at last. He shut off his chain saw and gave the thumb's up, stop work signal to his co-workers. Almost immediately, the great pine forest grew silent as all six of the crew's snarling saws were idled. Walton stretched his weary back and rubbed his shoulders. It had been a long, hard day.

Walton's foreman, Mike Rogers, dropped the tailgate on his beat-up 1965 crew-cab pickup, and the tree cutters slid their saws into the bed of the truck. Dusk was filtering through the forest; the air was growing nippy. The men were glad to be heading back to town, to hot suppers and a good night's rest. They had no way of knowing that this night, Wednesday, November 5, 1975, would be the longest, most terrifying night of their lives.

For Travis Walton, the ordeal he was about to undergo would be the most traumatic of his life, an experience so incredibly unique that he may be the only person on the planet, or certainly one of the very few, to have lived through it.

Walton and his fellow loggers, Steve Pierce, Allen Dalis, Kenneth Peterson, Dwayne Smith and John Goulette, were members of a tree-thinning crew working on a fuel-reduction strip in the Apache-Sitgreaves National Forest. For nine hours every day, they selectively cut down scores of small trees in an area where the forest had grown into a dense, potential fire hazard. The downed trees then had to be dragged into firebreaks and heaped together in piles which would eventually be burned under controlled conditions by the Forest Service.

Tree-thinning is dangerous and physically demanding work, but the day doesn't end when there is no longer enough light to continue cutting. After the chain saws, gas cans and lunch pails are loaded into the truck, there is still that long, rut-road drive back to civilization. For Mike Rogers' crew, that road was 15 bumping, bouncing miles. The primitive track switchbacks its way down from the Mogollon Rim to Arizona Highway 277. From there, it is another 32 miles to the small town of Snowflake.

All of the tree cutters were young. Rogers, the oldest of the team, was only 28. As always at this time of day, everyone was tired to the bone. But tiredness rarely robs the young of their exuberance or their sense of humor. They kidded Rogers about his decrepit pickup and his driving ability. They shouted, "Thank you, ma'am!" each time the truck slammed over a bump in the road.

Walton was sitting by the window on the passenger side of the front seat, rocking back and forth, watching the bobbing circles of light probing the darkness ahead of the pickup. Just for a split second, he caught a glimpse of a bright light shining through the tops of the pines. Within an instant, it was gone, blocked out by the dark branches of the great trees the truck was passing. The other members of the crew were still laughing and joking, urging Rogers to "pedal faster." Moments later, the light became visible again, and now it had Walton's total attention. What could it be? It was too early for the moon to have risen, and the moon had never shone that brightly. "What the hell *is* that?" he shouted. The others stopped talking.

Mike Rogers down-shifted, revved the truck up an incline in the road and abruptly slammed on the brakes at the edge of a small clearing. The entire open area was bathed in a soft, yellow glow, and above the glow, 15 feet off the ground, a large golden disc hung motionless in mid-air. "My God," Allen Dalis stammered. "It's a flying saucer!"

The luminous craft was shaped like two pie pans pressed together rim to rim, with a round dome on the top. It appeared to be about 15 to 20 feet in diameter and between eight and ten feet thick. No hatches, ports or windows were visible on its smooth, seamless metallic hull. It was as eerily silent as the forest below it. For one long, suspended moment, the young loggers stared in awe at this unbelievable sight. Then Travis Walton, who had opened the door on his side of the truck so he could lean out for a better look, swung out of the pickup and took his first tentative step in the direction of the saucer.

"Travis!" Rogers called in a loud whisper. "What the hell do you think you're doing? Get back here!"

Walton paused only momentarily before dropping into a crouch. He moved forward. He knew this was a once-in-a-lifetime experience, and he wanted to get as close as possible. Cautiously, he entered the circle of light directly below the space ship. Just as he heard someone in the truck behind him, say "That crazy son of a bitch," a noise began emanating from above. The sound was barely audible at first, a low mechanical hum which quickly grew in intensity and volume. The ship, though it remained stationary, began wobbling slightly. The noise it emitted became a roar as loud as a dozen turbine generators cranking up.

Walton was thoroughly frightened now. He turned to run, but in that split second, a blinding, bluish ray of light flashed down from the craft and struck him directly on the head and shoulders. As Kenneth Peterson would say later: "Travis went flying like he'd touched a live wire." The electrifying force from the ray threw Walton ten feet across the ground and knocked him unconscious.

In the pickup, everyone was yelling at once. "It got him! It killed him! Let's get outta here or we're next!"

Rogers, realizing his first responsibility was to save the lives of the rest of his crew, jammed the truck into low gear and peeled out in a spray of rocks and dirt. For several miles, he drove recklessly down the rut road, crashing through roadside bushes and glancing off boulders as he tried to watch both the road and the rear-view mirrors for signs of pursuit. At last, when Highway 277 came into sight, he hit the brakes.

"You can get out here," he told his crew. "You should be safe now. I'm goin' back to get Travis."

The still-panicked men raised a clamor: "Mike, that's crazy! That thing could still be there! It'll kill you like it killed him!"

"We don't know for sure that Travis is dead," Rogers answered. "I'm goin' back and pick him up. That's what we should have done in the first place."

The initial shock of the terrifying experience was wearing off. The men were calming down. One by one, they all volunteered to accompany their foreman back into the dark woods. Rogers drove much more carefully this time while his crew scanned the black sky for any sign of light. When they reached the clearing, the UFO was gone. But so was Travis Walton. Timorously, the men stepped out of the truck, leaving the engine running and the doors open. Warily they explored the area with the beam of a single flashlight. They shouted Travis' name into the cold darkness and listened in vain for a reply. "We're goin' to have to get some help," said Rogers. "Let's go to town and call the sheriff."

On the way, the crew argued over what they should tell the authorities. Would anyone believe them if they said their friend had been zapped by a flying saucer, and then vanished without a trace? On the other hand, if they concocted a more plausible tale, it wouldn't stand up for any length of time and might even hamper the search. They all finally agreed there was only one thing to do: tell the truth right from the start. Mike Rogers parked his truck in front of a payphone in the tiny hamlet of Heber, west of Snowflake. Ken Peterson dialed the Navajo County Sheriff's Department. He told the dispatcher only that a member of their logging crew was lost, and that they needed immediate help.

Within a remarkably short time, a shiny brown car pulled up alongside the pickup. A tall, formidable-looking law enforcement officer got out. "Okay, what's the problem here?" he asked bluntly. Clumsily, Rogers tried to explain that a friend of theirs was missing in the forest, that he was hurt, probably badly, maybe dead. The deputy's eyes narrowed. "All right, start at the beginning," he said.

As calmly and coherently as possible, the loggers told the deputy exactly what had taken place. The officer's hard eyes moved from face to face as the workers spoke, but he remained silent after they finished.

"You don't believe us, do you?" Rogers asked.

"I'm not saying I do or I don't," the deputy answered. "But if somebody is hurt up on that ridge, we better get a move on." He radioed the sheriff's office and quickly filed a missing person report.

It took a little over an hour for Sheriff Marlin Gillespie and Undersheriff Ken Coplan to bring a spotlight-equipped, four-wheel drive pickup to Heber. Accompanied by Rogers, Peterson and Dalis as guides, they drove to the site of the encounter. For several hours, four of the men searched the immediate area with flashlights while the other two drove over as much of the surrounding network of logging trails as possible. Around midnight, they rendezvoused in the clearing. Gillespie concluded they had done all they could for the night. He directed everyone to return to town to help organize a full-scale search which would begin at daybreak.

"Somebody's got to break the news to Travis' mom," Rogers said. "I guess that's up to me."

"I'll go with you," Undersheriff Coplan offered.

Travis Walton's mother, Mary Kellett, is a remarkable woman, strong, independent and resourceful. After her divorce, she had raised her six children on her own and was currently living alone outside the tiny community of Overgard, east of Heber. Rogers and Coplan pulled into her yard at one in the morning. The house was dark, of course, but when they stepped up on the porch, they heard Mary Kellett's voice from behind the door. "That's far enough."

They knew right away her watchdog had awakened her, and they suspected she had a Winchester aimed at them. After the two men quickly identified themselves, she lowered the rifle and unlocked the door. As she lit a Coleman lantern, she asked, "It's about Travis, isn't it?"

"Yes ma'am," Rogers nodded. He proceeded to describe carefully what had happened. Kellett maintained her composure as the strange tale unfolded, then she said, "I'd better call Duane."

Duane Walton is one of Travis' older brothers. He had been the most steadfast, responsible member of the family, the one everyone always relied on when the going got tough. Duane is tall and muscular, an amateur boxer, rodeo bull rider and horseshoer who was presently attending college in Phoenix. Since Mary Kellett had no phone in her house, she asked Coplan and Rogers to drive her to the home of her daughter, Allison Neff.

There she placed the call to Duane. In her straight forward manner, she told him, "You better get up here right away. It looks like a flying saucer got Travis." One can only speculate what the impact of such a message might be on someone suddenly awakened at three in the morning. But without hesitation, Duane Walton and his wife, Carol, got dressed and headed for Snowflake.

At dawn on November 6, a large search party composed of the sheriff's posse, the U.S. Forest Service and the Navajo County Search and Rescue Team rolled out of Heber and into the woods. Other searchers soon arrived from Holbrook. Throughout the day they conducted a very systematic sweep of the entire area between Highway 277 and the Mogollon Rim. Not a trace of Travis Walton was found, not even a scrap of clothing snagged on a branch, nor a single footprint.

Sheriff Gillespie ordered the search to be resumed in the morning, but everyone was now facing the cold reality that they would be searching for a corpse; an injured person stood little chance of surviving two freezing nights in the depths of those wild woods. And, inevitably, a more ominous thought was also creeping into some minds. A tired, angry forest ranger voiced the suspicion of all when he confronted the young loggers, demanding to know where they had hidden the body.

The crew reacted with shock and outrage. Duane Walton had to step into the shouting match to calm things down, although at this point, even he was not sure the accusation was false.

The search party that went out on Friday morning was larger than that of the previous day, but, again, nothing was found. This time, the searchers dug into the piles of downed trees, rolled over logs and inspected any other place where a body could be concealed. It was all a waste of time. Gillespie now wanted to call off the search, but the Walton family convinced him to try once more. The final effort utilized every resource available in Navajo County, a helicopter, several private planes and teams of horsemen, but they all might just as well have stayed at home.

During the early stages of the search, Gillespie tried to keep the UFO aspect of the case from being publicized. As could be expected, word got out all too quickly anyway. By Saturday night, dozens of journalists and TV news crews were converging on tiny Snowflake. William Spaulding, a UFOlogist from

Phoenix's Ground Saucer Watch, arrived in time to take electromagnetic readings in the trees and bushes at the saucer site. He reported finding an abnormally high magnetic field in the area, along with residual traces of ozone.

By that time, the local law enforcement officials were rapidly losing interest in the long-vanished, perhaps non-existent UFO. They were more concerned about the very real possibility that they had a homicide on their hands. Gillespie asked the six tree-cutters if they would volunteer to take lie detector tests. They all readily agreed to do so.

The tests were given by the Arizona Department of Public Safety's polygraph examiner, Cy Gilson, Monday morning in the County Courthouse in Holbrook. Each man's test lasted at least an hour, during which time they were asked if they had killed or injured Travis Walton and whether or not they had actually seen a UFO. In his preliminary evaluation, Gilson stated that the charts showed five of them men had passed the tests. Allen Dalis' test had to be ruled "inconclusive," since he was still in an extremely agitated state of mind. When Gilson released his official report, he concluded: "These polygraph examinations prove that these five men did see some object they believe to be a UFO."

The logging crew was greatly relieved by this vindication, but for the Walton family, it was cold comfort at best. They were sure now that Travis had not been murdered by his fellow workers, but his fate was still unknown. For all they knew, Travis had literally vanished from the face of the earth. Although the family members were nearing the point of exhaustion, they all slept fitfully that Monday night. Then at five minutes after midnight, the phone rang at Travis' sister's home.

Allison Neff's husband, Grant, sleepily answered the call, and instantly came fully awake when he heard the voice on the other end of the line. It was Travis; the first words he uttered were: "They brought me back."

Travis' voice was strained and toned with hysteria. He was gasping as if he had been running wildly. "Where are you?" Grant asked. Travis mumbled something about the payphone outside the Enco station in Heber, now closed for the night.

"Stay right where you are, Travis," Grant said, firmly. "Don't go anywhere. I'll get Duane and we'll be there as soon as we can."

Grant sped off to Mary Kellett's house, picked up Duane and the two of them drove at once to Heber. When they reached the phone booth, it appeared to be empty. Then they realized Travis was crouched on the floor with his arms wrapped around his shins, his head pressed against his knees. He looked up when Duane opened the door. Relief shone in his fear-filled eyes. As Duane lifted him to his feet, he began to babble almost incoherently: "They were horrible... white skin... huge eyes. God, those eyes!"

"Don't try to talk now, Travis," Duane said gently. "Let's get you in the pickup where it's warm."

During the drive back to Snowflake, Travis looked at his watch. "It's... after midnight," he gasped. "I must have been inside that ship at least two hours." Grant and Duane glanced at one another uncomfortably.

"Travis," Duane said carefully. "You were gone for five days."

"Five days? That can't be —not five days. Aw, no." Travis ran his hand over the heavy stubble on his chin and fell silent for the rest of the trip. In Snowflake, he was tearfully, happily reunited with his family members who never expected to see him alive again. After everyone's joyous emotions ran their course, Duane Walton firmly took charge of the situation.

He could see clearly that his brother was in no condition yet to undergo questioning by either law enforcement officials or the press. He also believed an immediate medical examination was imperative, but not by a local doctor. If the family agreed, he would take Travis to Phoenix for examination. He would stay at Duane and Carol's home there for the time being. Having been harassed nearly to the limits of their tolerance by the media, curiosity-seekers and moronic prank callers, the family endorsed that plan. Duane asked Travis to change clothes. When he had done so, his work clothes were placed in paper sack for future testing. Travis seemed extremely dehydrated —he drank glass after glass of water— so Duane asked him to fill a jar with a urine sample. Next, he had Travis step on the bathroom scales. His weight had dropped from 165 pounds to 154.

Before dawn, Duane and Travis left for Phoenix, completing the drive by early morning. While the exhausted abductee lay down to try to sleep, his brother called William Spaulding, the UFOlogist he thought he could trust, to ask his advice as to a good doctor. This proved to be a mistake. Spaulding, apparently hoping to become the central figure in the upcoming media storm, informed the media that Travis Walton had returned. Almost immediately, Duane Walton's phone began ringing off the wall.

Duane warded off the callers by telling them Travis was in a Tucson hospital and could not be disturbed. The one caller he should not have hung up on was Coral Lorenzen. Lorenzen, along with her husband, James, is one of the nation's foremost UFO investigators. She was then secretary-treasurer of the Tucson-based Aerial Phenomena Research Organization (APRO) and co-author of several meticulously researched books on UFOs. Lorenzen quickly phoned every hospital in Tucson and the surrounding area. She then called Duane again and flatly asked, "Is Travis with you. Because, Mr. Walton, if he is, I believe I can be of help." She explained that she could get two physicians associated with APRO to make a discreet house call by mid-afternoon. Perhaps Duane sensed the sincerity in her voice; he accepted her proposal.

Coral Lorenzen, accompanied by Doctors Joseph Saults and Howard Kendell, arrived at Duane's home at 3:30 p.m. After Duane made it clear that because of Travis' distressed condition, there would be no interviews nor photographs taken, the doctors performed a very thorough physical. To everyone's relief, the young man showed no signs of harm beyond a small red spot on his right arm, which he thought might have been caused by a thorn or branch during his last day at work.

Travis spent another restless night repeatedly awakened by nightmare images of white, spongy faces with enormous eyes hovering over him.

The following afternoon, a more than slightly exasperated Sheriff Gillespie showed up and vividly expressed his anger at not having been informed of Travis' return. When he saw Travis lying weary and pale on the davenport, Gillespie apologized. "Sheriff," Travis said weakly, "I want to take a lie detector test, just like my buddies did." Gillespie promised to make the necessary arrangements and left.

The crowd of reporters besieging the Walton resident in Phoenix was steadily growing larger. The phone seemed never to stop ringing. Duane's patience was wearing very thin. Then Coral Lorenzen called again. She told him a team of investigators from the *National Enquirer* was in town and had contacted APRO in the hope of setting up a meeting with Travis. It might be worth talking to them, Lorenzen said, for they had a proposal that could help take the media pressure off.

Duane was very skeptical about talking to representatives of such a sensational tabloid, but his curiosity got the better of him. He decided to meet with them in his driveway. When the *National Enquirer* team arrived, they found Duane leaning against his pickup with his muscular arms folded across his chest. He greeted the visitors by saying, "Nobody's goin' to laugh at my brother."

The *National Enquirer* team took an immediate disliking to Duane Walton. One of the reporters, Jeff Wells, would later write: "He was one of the meanest, toughest looking men I'd ever seen —eyes full of nails, tense, unpredictable."

"We have no intention of laughing at your brother," Wells nervously clarified. "In fact, we are here to make sure no one laughs at him. Our editor has authorized us to move the two of you to a hotel where unwanted visitors will be turned back at the desk, and only the calls you wish to receive will be forwarded to your room. This evening, we'd like to bring by a group of UFO experts from APRO to talk to Travis about his experience."

"Wait here," Duane said. He went inside to confer with Travis and soon returned to say, "We'll take you up on that offer." Shortly thereafter, the Walton brothers moved into the Scottsdale Sheraton Inn.

That night, the *Enquirer* team brought seven people to the suite. Introductions were made all around. There was James Lorenzen, APRO's international director; James Harder, APRO's director of research; and five doctors: Howard Kendell, Joseph Saults, Robert Ganelin, Jean Rosenbaum and Beryl Rosenbaum.

James Lorenzen's first impression of Travis Walton was that his "demeanor resembled that of a caged bobcat." His eyes moved quickly and suspiciously from person to person. His handshake was limp and timid. The cynical Jeff Wells decided he was either scared to death or was a brilliant actor. James Harder sat down beside Travis to explain in a quiet, reassuring voice that he no longer had anything to fear. He promised that the people in the room were capable of understanding what he had been through.

Harder suggested the easiest, most accurate way for Travis to relate his traumatic experience to them would be under hypnosis. To demonstrate how this would be done, Harder asked Lorenzen to allow himself to be hypnotized while Travis watched. When the demonstration ended, Travis was visibly relaxed. He settled back comfortably and let Harder gently put him into a state of regressive hypnosis. As everyone in the crowded, hushed suite listened intently, Travis Walton began to re-live the night of November 5.

He moaned loudly. He was suffering excruciating pain, lapsing in and out of consciousness, unable to raise his arms or focus his eyes. He could see light around him in a blurry whiteness within which shadowy shapes were moving. There seemed to be a curved ceiling above him. "A hospital," he thought. "That's it. I'm lying in a hospital. There are doctors standing around me." Then, his vision cleared, and he gasped out loud. The three creatures leaning over him were definitely not doctors.

They were humanoid in form, with two legs, two

arms, and small delicate five-fingered hands. Their heads were hairless, white-skinned, and overly large for their bodies. Travis described them as resembling human fetuses five feet in height. Their craniums bulged like mushrooms above their small, under-sized faces, and their eyes were enormous, glassy bubbles. The huge, brown irises were so large that very little white showed around the edges. When the creatures blinked, their eyelids slid down and snapped back up, like those of salamanders.

Travis panicked. He sat up and struggled unsteadily to his feet. A wide, metalic device encircling his chest clattered to the floor as he crashed against a tray spread with strange utensils. Frantically, he pushed the closest alien away with his hand, feeling a soft, spongy flesh beneath its coverall-like garment. He was shouting now: "Get away from me! What are you? Let me out of here!" The creatures moved toward him with their hands outstretched. Travis groped desperately through the instruments on the table, seeking a weapon. His hand closed around a thin, transparent, 18-inch cylinder which he raised in a threatening gesture.

"And then?" James Harder asked softly.

The hypnotized Travis Walton was trembling, speaking in gasps; "They backed off. Went through an open door. Turned right. Disappeared."

Travis said he glanced around the small room, hoping to see another door or a hatch through which he could escape. There was nothing, only smooth, grey metal walls approximately seven feet high. The room was lighted by a single, translucent, two-inch column smoothly embedded in the ceiling. The air was heavy and hard to breathe. With the pain still throbbing in his head and chest, he stepped cautiously through the doorway. Since the aliens had gone to the right, Travis moved quietly to the left, inching his way along a three-foot wide, circular corridor until he reached another open door. Beyond this door was a round, empty room in the center of which stood a single, high-backed, gracefully molded, one-legged chair.

Travis told how he approached it warily. As he crossed the room, a bizarre thing happened. The grey walls turned black, and multitudes of tiny pinpoints of light shone through. It was, he said, as if he had entered a planetarium. He turned his attention back to the chair. On the end of the left arm, there was a short, thick, T-shaped lever. On the right arm, there was a miniature, green screen with a dozen or more buttons below it. The screen was criss-crossed with black lines intersected by short dashes.

Impulsively, Travis pushed one of the buttons; the linear pattern changed instantly. He eased himself into the chair, took hold of the T-lever, and rotated it slightly. The star-scape around him swerved suddenly down-ward, but stopped as soon as he put the handle back in its original position. "Quit foolin' around, man," he told himself. "You don't know *what* you're doin'." He rose from the chair and turned to re-cross the room. But there in the doorway stood a human being.

The man was tall, with sandy-blond hair and a clean-shaven face. He was wearing a transparent spherical helmet, a tight-fitting blue suit, a black belt, and black boots. And he was smiling. Travis let out a great sigh of relief. "An astronaut," he thought. "An American astronaut."

He ran forward spewing out a stream of questions. "Where am I? Can you help me? Can you get me out of..." He stopped in mid-sentence as he got a closer look at the face in the fish bowl-like globe. A chill ran through him. "I don't know who this guy is," he thought. "But he's damn sure not from NASA."

The man's golden-hazel eyes were abnormally bright, and his facial expression never changed. Silently, he took Travis by the arm and firmly but gently led him through a door, down a ramp, and into a large hangar-like enclosure. Glancing back, Travis saw the ship from which they had emerged was identical to the one he saw in the woods, except that it was nearly three times as big. Two smaller craft were sitting nearby.

The "human" took Travis down a wide hallway to a rectangular room where three more figures stood —two men and a woman. They were similar in appearance to the first man with the same clothing, expressions and fixed smiles, but they wore no helmets. Travis tried to speak to them, but they simply continued to smile as they guided him to a shiny, black table. They lifted him onto the edge of the table and pressed him down on his back. The woman bent over him, her long hair falling over her shoulders. In her hand was an object resembling a clear, soft-plastic oxygen mask. Travis tried to rear up, the the woman deftly placed the mask over his mouth and nose. At once, he grew weak; his vision blurred and everything went black.

Travis Walton's next memory was that of lying on cold pavement at the edge of a highway in the pine-scented Arizona night. A bright light was shining above him. He pushed himself up just in time to see a great, silvery disc hover momentarily over the road before it shot up vertically and disappeared among the stars. Travis scrambled to his feet and ran non-stop to the payphone in Heber.

"Everything is all right now," James Harder said, and Travis came out of the hypnotic trance. He was emotionally drained by having re-lived the pain and fear of his astonishing experience. The *Enquirer* reporters were eager to bombard him with further questions, but Duane emphatically informed them that was all for the evening. He ushered everyone out of the suite, and Travis was to spend another restless night in dream-filled sleep.

In the morning, Harder brought John J. McCarthy of the Arizona Polygraph Laboratory to the hotel to perform the lie detector test Travis had requested. Harder expressed strong misgivings about having the test administered so soon. He feared that Travis' still-agitated state of mind would render the results inconclusive at best, or end in failure at worst. Travis was, indeed, still very confused; he was even having trouble remembering what day it was. But he insisted on going ahead with the test, so Harder acquiesced, against his better judgement.

For more than an hour, Travis Walton answered either yes or no to a long series of questions about himself, his past, and his recent traumatic encounter. When the test was concluded, McCarthy flatly, and somewhat contemptuously stated, "Travis, your responses are deceptive. You're not telling the truth."

"I... I am telling the truth," the tape recording of the conversation reveals Travis as responding. "There must be some mistake. Will you... ah... test me again?"

"There is no need to go any further," replied McCarthy. "I've got my answers." He packed up his equipment and left.

Travis was stunned by the outcome of the test, but Harder tried to reassure him by saying that lie detectors measure and record stressful physiological reactions: they do not measure lies *per se*. He felt the test showed only that Travis needed more time to recover from his ordeal. Let sometime go by, Harder advised, then schedule a second testing.

A disappointed *National Enquirer* team left town the next day. On December 16, the tabloid ran a cover story titled: "5 Witnesses Pass Lie Test While Claiming Arizona Man Captured by UFO". The article made no mention of Travis' failure to pass his test.

December was a busy month for Travis Walton. He accepted offers to appear on talk shows in both the United States and Canada, and he told his story to Leonard Nimoy in the pilot episode of a television show called "The Unexplained." By February 1976, he felt more than confident enough to take a second polygraph test. During the previous three months, he, Duane and Mary Kellett had frequently been accused of perpetrating a hoax, so both Duane and Mary also volunteered to be tested. The new tests were performed by George Pfeifer, a charter member of the Arizona Polygraph Association.

Asked whether he had seen a UFO, had been struck by a bluish ray, had seen strange beings in a strange room, Travis answered "yes." When asked if he had conspired with anyone to perpetrate a hoax in this matter, he answered "no." Duane Walton was asked if he had participated in a hoax to pretend Travis was missing, whether he knew where Travis was located during that period, and whether Travis hid on the Kellett Ranch. To each question, Duane answered "no". Mary Kellett answered "no" when she was asked if she had conspired with Travis or any person to perpetrate a hoax, whether she had concealed Travis from public contact, or knew where her son was between November 5 and November 11, 1975. On the basis of the answers, George Pfeifer gave his opinion that both of the young men and their mother had answered all the questions truthfully, and had not attempted to be deceptive in any way. At last, Travis and Duane Walton, Mary Kellett and the APRO representatives who had stood behind them felt vindicated. Their sense of relief was short-lived, however, for the controversy over the validity of this close encounter had only begun.

Soon, America's number one UFO debunker, Phillip Klass, entered the dispute. Klass flatly and emphatically does not believe in UFOs. He has built a considerable reputation writing books and articles about his investigations and dismissals of UFO sightings. He surely relished the opportunity to tear apart the most highly-publicized UFO story of the 1970s. But he didn't bother traveling to Snowflake to meet personally with the participants, as APRO's investigators had done. He merely conducted interviews with a limited number of people by long distance telephone calls.

Klass' first task was to try to discredit the second set of lie detector tests. He found it highly disturbing that Pfeifer allowed Travis and James Lorenzen to suggest some of the questions to be asked. He called this "a practically unheard of procedure." Pfeifer countered by saying his tests varied in no way from the accepted polygraph procedures he had always used when he was a detective-sergeant in Miami, Florida.

All eight of the people who had passed their tests challenged Klass to set up a new round of polygraph examinations to be administered by an expert of his own choosing. If they failed that third set of tests, they said they would pay all the expenses themselves. Klass reluctantly agreed, but then after stalling, backed out of the agreement.

At this time, William Spaulding, the UFO specialist who apparently was still fuming at having been pushed out of the limelight by APRO and the *National Enquirer*, had a vicious accusation: he told the press a doctor had informed him that Travis had obviously been "hallucinating on some kind of drug, probably LSD." That accusation was halted when the Waltons produced the urine sample that Duane had insisted on for Travis immediately after he emerged from his ordeal. The urinalysis, along with the blood tests, showed no traces of any drugs.

Drugs or no, Phillip Klass insisted Travis' experience was nothing but a vivid hallucination. Klass had long been suspicious of hypnotic testimony being accepted as a true re-living of a past event. He pointed out that, contrary to popular belief, some hypnotized subjects can willfully lie. Others confuse their fantasies with reality, totally believing they are telling the truth and in that way can be totally convincing to the hypnotist and other witnesses.

According to Klass, there is no way to determine if information obtained under hypnosis is an actual memory and not a fantasy, unless there is some means of independent verification. Where, Klass asked, was the independent verification in this case? Not one shred of physical evidence had been produced to prove that Travis' dream-like recollection was anything more than a subconscious manifestation. Klass admitted that Travis Walton believed what he said, but insisted that it had never happened.

Klass took his hypothesis a step further: the hallucination took place during the perpetration of a hoax pulled off by Travis Walton and Mike Rogers. Klass figured Rogers was looking for a way out of his current Forest Service contact so he could go on to more lucrative jobs. He needed an excuse, a reason to be able to say it was too dangerous to work in those woods. He invented the UFO story and got Travis so enamored of the tale that he had a hallucination about it, imagining himself inside a space craft.

Klass' theory was accepted by many people, including Robert Schiller of *Readers' Digest.* APRO's representatives who had spent numerous hours with Travis, his family and co-workers, found the explanation completely unacceptable and certainly lacking any type of "independent verification."

Mike Rogers scoffed at Klass' motive for a hoax. A Forest Service tree-thinning contract can be defaulted on without serious penalty or prejudice, completely eliminating the need for any far-fetched excuse. Rogers was well-aware of that fact, since he had defaulted on a contract a few years earlier and knew the procedure. The Forest Service already owed Rogers for three weeks' work on his present contract, so it was hardly in his best interest to risk losing his payment and jeopardizing his ability to meet his payroll. Would the rest of the crew participate in a fraud which might result in the loss of their paychecks?

It hardly seems possible that none of the other workers were aware that Rogers and Walton were pulling off a hoax. Therefore, either they, too, were part of the scheme, or they were witnesses to a genuine, completely unexpected aerial phenomenon. Their own polygraph tests established that five of the six of them *did* see an object which they believed to be a UFO —a brilliant light in the dark forest where no such light could possibly be. Steve Dalis, whose test was labeled "inconclusive," also swore he saw that same lighted object.

The debunkers and the pro-UFO people were totally at odds, but they did agree on one thing: undeniably Travis Walton had been missing for five days. If either side could prove where he was during that interval, the mystery would be solved.

Travis obviously was not out in the thoroughly-searched woods. The polygraph tests proved he was not hiding at his mother's ranch, nor was he hidden by Duane. Mike Rogers and his crew, since they were initially suspected of foul play, were under extremely close scrutiny by the police, the media and the townspeople. Yet not one clue of Travis' whereabouts was reported by anyone during his absence.

Nor can Travis' eleven-pound weight loss be explained. Would he hide somewhere without food?

Where was Travis Walton between November 5 and November 11, 1975? Even Travis cannot fully answer that question, since he was conscious for less than two hours during his incredible experience. Where was he taken, why and by whom? In 1978, he wrote: "What occurred inside the craft and the events surrounding my capture and return are not in the least self-explanatory. By themselves, these events do not seem to make much sense. A lot of questions have been asked of me concerning what it all meant. The answer to these questions is that I do not know."

Bibliography - Chapter 12

Lorenzen, Coral and Jim. **Abducted! Confrontations with Beings from Outer Space.** Berkeley, California. Berkeley Publishing Corporation. 1977.

Klass, Phillip. *Skeptical Inquirer.* Buffalo, New York. Spring, 1981.

Schiller, Robert. *Readers' Digest.* Pleasantville, New York. November 1977.

Walton, Travis. **The Walton Experience.** Berkeley, California. Berkeley Publishing Company. 1978.

Wells, Jeff. *Skeptical Inquirer.* Buffalo, New York. Summer, 1981.

13
New Age Magic in Sedona

"Sooner or later, we'll see you in Sedona" reads the opening line in a Sedona Chamber of Commerce brochure. And, for certain contemporary pilgrims —those seeking psychic energy, metaphysical enlightenment and spiritual vibrations— these words are almost prophetic. Sooner or later, they all will come to Sedona, Arizona, or their quests for a higher truth and a cleansed inner spirit will be forever unfulfilled.

Sedona is the pulsing heart of the New Age movement. Here, in the center of a breathtakingly beautiful landscape, this small, plush town is situated near four major vortexes, or "power spots," which constantly emit intense psychic vibrations. In no other place on earth have so many vortexes been discovered in such close proximity to one another.

It is said that the vortexes of Sedona are so powerful that their energy permeates the entire Oak Creek

Canyon area, affecting the lives of everyone who comes near them. Nevertheless, the most obvious aura in this wealthy, strung-out-along-the-highway town is the smell of money.

In 1978, Sedona was just a sleepy little art colony with a population of 2,022 people. But with the coming of the New Age movement and publicity for the vortexes, its population jumped to 15,000 within a decade. Today, scores of brand-new mansions perch on the hillsides below the great towers of red sandstone. The town's streets are lined with trendy, expensive shops and restaurants. Traffic is often bumper-to-bumper as tourists throng into the bustling community for the community's ambience and Oak Creek Canyon's magnificence. Most people come simply to enjoy the plush resort town atmosphere, but others —the ones who hope to find something more than just a $100 motel room with a view or a good cup of frozen yogurt— have higher expectations.

They come to touch the vortexes. Or, more accurately, to let the vortexes touch them.

Vortex tours are big business in Sedona. All day long, brightly colored jeeps, loaded with eager pilgrims, shuttle back and forth from one New Age mecca to another. A good many of Sedona's visitors prefer to avoid the guided tours and approach the vortexes on their own, hoping to spend a few moments alone, absorbing the astonishing energy that emanates from the ancient rocks.

Why? What can one expect to experience by sitting, totally relaxed in a sandstone alcove? Just what, really, is a vortex?

Sedona poet Saundra Hodge likens the vortexes to invisible whirlpools that swirl out rather than down, while emitting "silent sounds." Science writer William

Corliss believes they are deviations and irregularities in the earth's magnetic field. New Age lecturer Dick Sutphen says, in his frequent psychic seminars in Sedona, that they are to the earth what accupressure points are to the human body. There are two types of vortexes in this world —positive and negative. The positive, or "light" power spots increase and externalize the energy being discharged from certain points on the surface of the planet, while negative "dark" vortexes destroy or reverse this energy. Vortexes are located in a number of places around the globe, but the most powerful concentrations exist only in four widely separated locations. Two are considered to be very negative and very dangerous: the Bermuda Triangle and Stonehenge in Sussex County, England. The strongest cluster of positive vortexes emanate from the Hawaiian island of Kauai, and from four large rock formations south and northwest of Sedona.

Positive vortexes produce three different kinds of energy, according to New Age practitioners. The Bell Rock and Airport Mesa sites release electrical energy which can stimulate the mind and elevate one's consciousness. The Cathedral Rock vortex is magnetic in nature, and creates a vibrational field or frequency that increases one's psychic perceptions since it acts primarily upon the subconscious mind. But it is the fourth vortex, the one in Boynton Canyon, that has the strongest positive force of the four. This vortex's energy is electromagnetic, said to be a perfectly balanced confluence of both vibrational frequencies.

If one accepts the existence of these invisible sources of power, what is to be expected from direct contact with a Sedona vortex? For the devotees of New Age thinking, almost anything can happen. When an "enlightened" New Ager sits in a quiet state of total relaxation within a vortex, anything is possible.

Trances are common occurrences. During a vor-
tex-induced trance, people may recall past lives and
see themselves as they were during a previous existence. One Sedona woman who calls herself Tanzara
discovered she has been reincarnated many times in
Egypt. She was also once a very rich woman in Austria,
and had been an Indian chief's wife. In her current life,
she is a cleaning lady. Intense visions may arise within
which apparitions become visible, and ghostly voices
are heard. This, the believers claim, is due to the fact
that places have memories just as people do. If a person can reach a state of total harmony with a special
landscape feature, it is possible to see images, hear
sounds, and feel emotions from the distant past. Spirits from other parts of the land are drawn to Sedona's
vortexes, too, and if a person's consciousness is high
enough, these spirits can be channeled.

A woman in Sedona professes to channel John
Lennon; she swears the deceased rock hero has spo-
ken through her on many occasions. Another channel-
er, known as Yananda, often delivers messages from
his "space brothers," whose craft has been sighted
above Bell Rock, absorbing the site's energy. A popular
local joke says that even though Sedona has no television station, it still has 80 channels.

Objects taken by visitors to a vortex can also be
altered by the radiating powers. Sutphen tells of a
woman from Virginia who meditated in the Boynton
Canyon vortex with her deceased father's watch
cupped in her hands. The battery in the watch had
been dead for months, but almost immediately the
timepiece began to tick again and has kept perfect time
ever since.

Claims are made that visiting a vortex can be

beneficial to a person's health. Some visitors report the symptoms of colds and flu disappear after a trip to a vortex. Others say they underwent a physical change that substantially eliminated their need for sleep.

A few have apparently absorbed sufficient power and New Age consciousness that they are able to walk barefoot on beds of hot coals as if they were taking a quick stroll on a moist pathway covered with cool moss. These Sedona fire-walks have been witnessed by many people, and televised by a CBS News team. Observers saw no signs of trickery. The fire-walkers believe their minds can make their bodies do whatever they ask of them. If walking on fire is no problem, other tasks or challenges may not seem so impossible.

Can there actually be cosmic forces so strong and complex that miraculous events of this sort are possible and believable? And, if so, where does this energy come from? How does it travel?

Some New Age thinkers have attempted to answer those questions through the application of geomantic theories. Geomancy, in its broadest sense, is the study of the earth's spirit. By determining the relationship of the natural landscape features with the underground currents beneath them and the celestial bodies above, it is allegedly possible to measure the spiritual dimensions of any part of the world.

Since nearly all earthly landscapes have been altered in one way or another by human activities —by roads, cities, farms, battles, cemeteries or temples— this, too, must be taken into consideration. The impact of human hands upon the land is always quite obvious, but the impact of the human mind on the natural world is much more difficult to perceive.

In times long past, there was a greater recognition of the interaction between the universal human spirit and the cosmic pulse of the earth. The Australian aborigines' Dreamtime ancestors certainly understood this relationship, as did the ancient Chinese, the Tibetans and the Mayans. Clearly the early Native Americans were much aware not only of the land's influence on the human mind, but of the effects of human thoughts and actions as well. During certain times and at special places, the psychic qualities of the physical environment can be influenced by human thoughts. Thus, when contemporary searchers seek to rediscover the long-lost psychic wisdom of vanished cultures, they turn to the branch of geomancy known as geomythics to explore the myths and stories which describe the historic events that determine a landmark's special character.

A study of Indian creation myths is often very helpful in this search. Place names may provide many clues to the spiritual qualities of the landscape affected by past events. Many mountains in the Southwest were considered sacred by the first people to inhabit the region; they often gave special mountains the names of Indian deities. When the Spanish came, they, too, sensed the holiness of these peaks and changed the mountains' names to those of Catholic religious figures. Perhaps the San Francisco Peaks, 40 air-miles north of Sedona's vortexes, may be linked to the age-old power grid.

Geomythicists have evolved an interesting, albeit unproven, theory about the connection between the San Francisco Peaks and the power spots around Sedona. They believe a vertical fault has split its way down from the center of the great crater surrounded by the rugged peaks. This deep geologic crack, along with others below the nearby Sunset Crater and the Wupakti Caves, have opened passageways into enormous,

BELL ROCK. This "beacon-vortex" of energy has convinced many that it transmits healing forces and strong emotions from the distant past.

water-filled caverns in the Precambrian layer of the earth's strata.

Reputedly, this underground reservoir is so huge that it responds to the pull of the moon, causing these holes to inhale and exhale air from the surface of the land at regular intervals. This air also is believed to travel laterally between the Precambrian level and the Redwall Limestone layer above it. Just south of Sedona, this earth-breath is blocked by an abrupt shift in the earth's crust which brought the Precambrian strata up to ground level. From this point, the air can flow no further, so it releases itself as electrical or magnetic energy from the antenna-like rock formations in and around Oak Creek Canyon. This sort of theorizing gives rise to an obvious question: how could such a conversion from air to energy take place?

In the minds of some, at least part of the answer is attributed to quartz crystals buried in the region. Partially exposed crystals have been discovered in the wind-sculpted, water-smoothed sandstone, so it seems logical to assume many more are emanating their energy from deep inside the rocks.

At Bell Rock, adherents of crystal power have dangled pendants over the vortex and concluded that there is a very large upright crystal somewhere below the surface of the ground. Bell Rock is an electrical "beacon-vortex" which shoots its energy straight down from the crown of the formation to the vortex, creating a "cone of power" which anyone can step into and absorb.

A first-time visitor to a vortex may well feel unsure how to approach such a strong source of mysterious power. Others, steeped in New Age rationale and in touch with their own inner spirit, seem to know intuitively what to do. The most commonly recommended procedure for the uninitiated is as follows: walk to the vortex and sit down. Breathe deeply, exhale slowly over and over to achieve total relaxation. Think of light. Hold out both hands, palms down, above the rock floor, and wait.

Some visitors following this procedure go into trances or see visions, but more likely the novice will feel a mild but very real tingle over the palms and along the fingers.

For every person who experiences at least that sensation, many other eager tourists scrambling on and around the vortexes will come away deeply disappointed and disillusioned that their hurried visit produced no striking effect. They are not alone in dismissing the vortex concept as complete nonsense.

Most members of conventional Christian churches are disdainful of New Age thinking, but they are uneasy over the movement's ever-expanding growth. A church minister in Sedona, Dana Willhelmsen, considers it "an ominous town," where a very eclectic collection of "irresponsible" people believe whatever they choose and pose a threat to traditional Christianity and society in general.

Other area residents agree. They express their distaste and contempt in a variety of ways. When hikers return to their cars after a vortex trip, they are likely to find a small flyer tucked under the windshield wiper, compliments of The Bohemian Brethren in nearby Jerome, Arizona. The flyer contains a derisive poem written in rap-song style:

> *So now you're a new age thinker.*
> *You swallowed the bait*
> *Hook, line and sinker.*
> *Trusting rocks that oscillate*
> *With herbs and chants, you meditate*

In a vortex with a crystal wand
Ascended master, you've been conned
If you think you're Christ
Better think twice
Open your eyes.
I'll give you a clue
There's only one God.
And He ain't you.

This amusing put-down of New Age believers is followed by a dead-serious list of Biblical quotes and references which describe the dreadful fates that will be suffered by those who stray from the paths of orthodox Christianity. Anyone entering "the gates that lead to destruction" by seeking knowledge beyond the revelations of the Bible can expect to spend an afterlife in "the lake which burneth with fire and brimstone."

But such scary warnings do little to deter committed New Agers. When you can walk on fire, hell may look a little different.

How to Visit the Vortexes of Sedona

All four vortex trips can begin at the uptown traffic light at the intersection of Highways 89A and 179, known locally as "The Y." To go to Bell Rock, drive south for five miles on 179. Just beyond the Forest Service's Bell Rock Rest Area, there are parking places on the left. From there, simply follow the well-worn paths to the base of the rock formation and walk up the sandstone until you reach the point where you can go no further without climbing the water-stained rocks.

Airport Mesa is also easily accessible. From "The Y," drive west one mile on Highway 89A, then turn left onto Airport Road. Just beyond the cattle guard, the path to the vortex lies to the left. It is located at the point where the second and third peaks converge. Watch for an oval indentation in the sandstone large enough to hold eight to ten people.

To reach Cathedral Rock, you have two choices. You can take 89A west from "The Y" for four and a half miles to a "Slow" sign and cattle guard. Before crossing the cattle guard, make a left onto a dirt road. Follow the signs to a parking area and picnic ground with a gate that is open from 9 a.m. to 8 p.m. Cathedral Rock is on the opposite side of Oak Creek, but if the water level is low enough, you can walk across to the vortex area.

The alternative approach, via Highway 179, does not require crossing Oak Creek. Head south from "The Y" past Bell Rock to Verde Valley School Road and drive west. The second half of this road is dirt, but four-wheel drive is not necessary. There is a parking area at Red Rock Crossing on Oak Creek. A bit of rugged uphill hiking is then necessary to enter this magnetic vortex.

The Boynton Canyon vortex is reached by driving west from "The Y" three miles to Dry Creek Road. Turn right and follow the road north for another three miles to a T-intersection. Go left for about a mile and a half and turn right at the fork. There is trailhead parking on the right side of the road from which two trails lead to this large electromagnetic vortex.

Sit down, breathe deep and relax. You never know what may happen.

Bibliography - Chapter 13

Corliss, William R. **Handbook of Unusual Natural Phenomena.** New York. Arlington House, Inc. 1977.

Mann, Nicholas R. **Sedona - Sacred Earth.** Prescott, Arizona. ZIVAH Publishing. 1989.

Sutphen, Dick. **Sedona: Psychic Energy Vortexes.** Malibu, California. Valley of the Sun Publishing

Company. 1986.

Transcript: *Secrets of Sedona*. New York. CBS News *48 Hours*, Show No. 146. Air date: March 27, 1991.

14

Flying Lizards
and Dancing Ghosts

Arizona has enough genuine mysteries, miracles and natural wonders that it hardly seems necessary for anyone to make up any tall tales about this fascinating state. But in Arizona, tall tales are almost as common as saguaros. And when an Arizonan starts telling whoppers, he or she can usually out-prevaricate the

235

best liars in all the other 49 states —Texas included.

Admittedly, Arizona's yarn spinners have a distinct advantage over the truth-twisters who live in our nation's milder regions. In Arizona, where the heat pops popcorn in the field and the air is so dry that postage stamps have to be stapled to envelopes, anything is possible and even the tallest tale can seem believable.

When a tourist asks why Arizona's water is so hard, the reply is apt to be: "If you think the water is hard here in town, you ought to go down to the river. The water there's so hard, you can't row a boat across it. It'll chew your oars to splinters." The tourist, having just downed a glass of Arizona water, may not find the story all that far-fetched.

Stories about the heat are equally easy to accept. Most newcomers are quite willing to believe that Arizona cowboys sit around campfires to cool off, or that most traffic jams are caused by melted asphalt.

Perhaps that plausibility factor explains why some otherwise hard-to-believe stories gain a degree of respectability when the setting is Arizona.

During the mid-1930s, a number of circuses traveling around the country were exhibiting miniature horses in their sideshows. These tiny ponies were no bigger than medium-sized dogs, and the plaid-suited pitchmen standing in front of the tents always shouted, "Step right up, ladies and gentlemen! See the world's smallest horses! Captured live in the Grand Canyon!"

Where these pint-sized ponies really came from is anybody's guess, but in an era when the earth's last and most remote places were being explored with startling discoveries, the general public could be forgiven if it fell for an occasional scam. After all, Komodo dragons and platypuses actually existed; was it unthinkable that a herd of pygmy horses might be living somewhere deep in the Grand Canyon? Motion pictures of that time reinforced this type of plausibility. King Kong had been discovered in the wilds of Africa, and another popular epic film, *The Lost World*, showed a colony of dinosaurs surviving on a hidden plateau in South America. Everyone knew King Kong was only a mechanical toy and the dinosaurs were just magnified lizards, but the notion of strange creatures existing in unexplored places intrigued even members of the scientific community.

The American Museum of Natural History took an interest in the pygmy horses in 1937. A few of the museum's scientists felt the ponies might be descendants of *eohippus*, The Dawn Horse. This small, early mammal had been extinct for 35 million years, but if a herd had somehow wound up completely isolated in a secluded, secure habitat —atop a mesa in the Grand Canyon for instance— their successors might still be there.

The scientists poured over the maps of the canyon and studied all the photographs they could find. They all agreed the high plateau known as Shiva Temple was the likeliest place to find a lost world. This mesa is detached from the rest of the landscape, buttressed by sheer walls and its crest is forested. The prospect of making a major paleontological discovery here was so irresistible that the American Museum of Natural History organized an expedition to Arizona to search for the Dawn Horse. When word of the proposed expedition appeared in newspapers around the country, Emory Kolb, the great Grand Canyon photographer, promptly called the museum to offer his services. He pointed out that no one was better qualified than he to be the official photographer since he knew the canyon intimately and had filmed it in all of its varied moods.

But the Dawn Horse team wasted no time in dismissing Kolb's offer. "Sorry, Mr. Kolb," they told him, "but you have no scientific background, no knowledge of paleontology and besides, you are in your later fifties. We fear this undertaking would be too strenuous for a man of your age."

Kolb put down the phone and tapped his fingers on the desk. "Too old, eh?" he fumed. "Well, if I can't join your little expedition, I guess I'll have to launch one of my own." Less than a week later, Emory Kolb hefted his tattered rucksack and tromped off to Shiva Temple. The climb was rather strenuous, but no more so than many other scrambles he had made in the past. Reaching the summit, he searched it diligently and found some newly-shed deer horns and sherds of ancient pottery, but no pygmy horses.

The view from the plateau was magnificent, so Kolb shot several rolls of film. The next morning, he created a small cairn of stacked rocks on the mesa's highest point. Although he was not ordinarily a litter-bug, he crumpled up the wrappers from his Eastman Kodak film and tossed them on the ground. How he must have chuckled as he climbed down the mesa, knowing that when the museum's expedition arrived, they would not only discover no pygmy horses, but would realize they were not even the first humans to ascend Shiva Temple.

But the elusive pygmy horses were not the first fantastic creatures thought to have inhabited Arizona's forbidding terrain. Over a hundred years ago, on June 7, 1890, the *Tombstone Epitaph* printed an astonishing story on its front page. "All of Tombstone was in an uproar yesterday," the article began, "when two cowboys rode in and bought implements to skin an enormous flying creature which they said they had killed on the desert between the Whetstone and the Huachuca Mountains."

The cowboys claimed to have won an epic battle against a giant, winged lizard. To back up their boast, they displayed one of the monster's wing tips, cut off as a souvenir. This strange, curved claw with a bit of flesh still attached was described by the author of the *Epitaph* article as resembling an extremely oversized bat wing tip. Had it not been for this curious piece of physical evidence, it is unlikely anyone would have given any credence to the cowboys' bizarre tale.

They said they had sighted the creature from a distance. There appeared to be something wrong with it, for it could only fly a few yards before coming down to rest with its beak open like an exhausted bird.

"After the first shock of wild amazement," the *Epitaph* account continued, "the two men, who were on horseback and armed with Winchester rifles, regained courage to pursue the monster and, after an exciting chase of several miles, succeeded in getting near enough to wound it with their rifles. The creature then turned on the men but, owing to its exhausted condition, they were able to keep out of its way and, after a few well-directed shots, the monster rolled over and remained motionless.

"It had an elongated eel-like body some 92 feet long. Its two legs were attached to the body in front of the wings. The 80-foot wings were of thick, translucent membrane devoid of hair or feathers. The head was about eight feet long with jaws thickly set with strong sharp teeth and giant protruding eyes the size of dinner plates. The men are reported to have made preparations to ship the hide east for scientific examination. The finders returned early this morning accompanied by several prominent men who will endeavor to bring the strange creature to this city before it is mutilated."

The *Epitaph* story was reprinted in the California newspapers for it was of considerable interest to the citizens of that state. Over a period of nearly 60 years, the people living in the vicinity of California's Lake Elizabeth reported frequent sightings of a huge flying reptile whose home was the lake itself. The earliest sightings were recorded by Don Pedro Carrillo, a Mexican land grantee who lived in the area during the 1830s. His writings described a fearsome beast he believed to be a manifestation of the devil. Carrillo also kept a tally of the livestock he lost to its depredations.

Frontier historian Major Horace Bell got a look at the monster in 1855. In his memoirs, he wrote: "It was midday, and the sun shone benignly on the mirror-like surface of the lake, which was as calm as a sleeping infant. Then, as terrifying as a peal of thunder from a clear sky, a great whistling, hissing, screaming roar issued from a growth of cattails on the margin of the lake. From our position, we could discern the outline of a huge monster with enormous bat-like wings. At times, it would flap these wings and splash the water as if attempting to rise from the mud where it lay."

Bell and his companions galloped off to the nearby Rivera ranch where they armed themselves with pistols, rifles and lariats. But when they returned to the lake, the monster was gone; its nauseous smell still dominated the area.

In later years, many other local people swore they, too, had seen the creature winging its way across the lake just at sundown. Once, Don Felipe Rivera managed to get close enough to the monster to empty his revolver at it, to no avail. By 1888, word of these encounters had become so widespread that an agent of the Sells Brothers Circus offered Rivera $20,000 if he could capture the thing alive. Rivera and his ranch hands fashioned large nets out of heavy ropes and headed for the lake. They reported that when they reached the shore, the monster burst out of the water and flew away to the east —toward Arizona— and was never seen again in California.

Of course, it sounds a little suspicious that the monster disappeared just as Don Felipe was being pressed to prove it really existed. Still, it is curious that a creature of an identical description was reportedly gunned down in an Arizona desert a year and a half later.

In 1970, a California-based organization called the Society for the Investigation of the Unexplained (SITU) took an interest in the eighty-year-old *Tombstone Epitaph* article. SITU wondered if there might have been any follow-up articles. A check with several local Tombstone history buffs revealed that there had indeed been a second article —accompanied by a printed photograph of the creature.

The photo, SITU's investigators were told, showed an enormous, bat-like monster strung up on the side of a barn with its wings spread out. In the foreground, six men posed with their arms outstretched, fingertip-to-fingertip, to show its size. The arm lengths of six men would be about 36 feet, far short of the 80 feet reported in the original story, but still far longer than the wing span of any living thing that has flown since prehistoric times.

Immediately, the SITU team asked if copies of the photograph still existed. No one was sure, but apparently a lot of early *Tombstone Epitaph* readers had clipped out that picture and kept it to show their grandchildren. A number of oldtimers clearly remembered having seen it during childhood, but no one knew who still had a copy. A search of the *Epitaph's* archives proved fruitless. The frontier newspaper had not made a concentrated effort to file all back issues, and those that remained had been treated with neglect over the years. The crucial issue was missing. Still, it remains possible that somewhere, in the long-unturned pages of an aged scrapbook, or in the bottom of a forgotten trunk in a dusty attic, the photograph is waiting to be rediscovered.

Stories of this sort leave one longing to have been present when the strange episodes took place —to have seen the cowboys doing battle with the winged lizard, to have helped dig up the ancient Roman swords outside Tucson, or to have seen Travis Walton step out of the flying saucer west of Heber. It seems that the more bizarre an event is, the fewer eye-witnesses there are.

But some of Arizona's mysteries linger on to be witnessed by thousands, such as the Ghost of Coal Mine Canyon.

When the full moon rises above a canyon east of Tuba City, the ghostly phenomenon will usually occur. The ghost appears on a rock formation across from a canyon tributary. It is a large, luminous figure which gradually increases in size, moves back and forth in a wraithlike dance until it vanishes in the darkness. It has been photographed and seen by countless numbers of spectators over the years.

The apparition has a legend attached to it. The chimera is said to be the spirit of an Indian woman who once loved a valiant warrior. After he was killed in a great battle in Coal Mine Canyon, she died of grief and still wanders in search of her dead lover. She

COAL MINE CANYON. When a full moon rises, an apparition dances across the canyon walls, gradually growing larger until it disappears.

Photo by LaDonna Kutz

dances forever on the top of the blunt spire known as The Ghost in her forlorn hope that the slain warrior will return to her.

Ask a Tuba City Navajo about the ghost and he or she is likely to answer: "I have heard of it, but I have never seen it. We are told not to go there, not to go near anything that can bewitch us."

The fact that the ghost has a natural explanation may not mean it lacks bewitching powers. The combination of interactions which produce the phenomenon is so rare it would be a "power spot" equal to any around Sedona.

When a summertime full moon is in the correct position in the sky, it shines its light through a side canyon onto the lonely spire. Heat waves stored in the earth rise to greet the moonlight, and the silvery, swirling dance begins. Whether or not this dance is really magical is anyone's call. But the least that can be said is that the Ghost of Coal Mine Canyon is definitely the most grandiose spook-light in the entire United States.

The fluorescent apparition might be an appropriate symbol for all of Arizona's mysteries: it tantalizes and perplexes just as the rest of her mysteries do. From the earliest of times to the present day, Arizona's mystique has hovered over this spellbound land like the shimmering heat wave that beckoned to young Hook. It waits —ever present, ever patient and ever ready— to reveal itself to anyone perceptive enough to sense that it is there. In a land so eternally enigmatic, who knows what is yet to come?

How to Visit the Ghost

The "Tuba City SE, Arizona" topographical map pinpoints the exact location of the phenomenon with the